POSITIVE IMPRESSIONS:
EFFECTIVE TELEPHONE SKILLS

A. W. (Tony) Hitt
with Kurt Wulff

AIM PRESS
division of
American Institute of Motivation, Inc.
514 Earth City Expressway
St. Louis, MO 63045

Cover design by Lee, Allen Advertising
Illustrations by Eric Wulff
Authors' photo by Ray Kersting

Library of Congress Cataloging-in-Publication Data

Hitt, A. W. (Tony), 1964-

Positive Impressions: Effective Telephone Skills
A. W. (Tony) Hitt with Kurt Wulff
p. cm.
Includes bibliographical references and index.
ISBN 1-881183-00-9
1. Telephone in business. 2. Telephone etiquette.
I. Wulff, Kurt. 1964- II. Title
HF5541.T4H58 1992 651.7'3--dc20 92-7858 CIP
Printed in USA

10 9 8 7 6 5 4 3 2 1

In memory of my grandfather, L. L. Hitt.
A copacetic man.

- A.W.H.

To my parents, Art and Judy, for their
lifelong encouragement and unwavering belief in my dreams.
To my wife, Missy, whose unconditional love and support
make my dreams a reality every day.

- K.C.W.

Acknowledgments

This book has truly been a team effort in both the vision and execution. That this book is now complete is a credit to each of the following individuals' selfless dedication to a common goal. These mentions are a fraction of the thanks they are owed.

To the past *"Positive Impressions"* seminar participants, who have generously taught us as much as we have taught them.

To our assistant, Lena Usery, who kept things together and running on those days when we needed more time on the book.

To Tona Court -- friend, mentor, and master editor -- for lending a critical eye when it was needed and in appreciation of her endless hours of debate on the correct placement of commas and the use of the proper tense.

To Ellen Hahn, for her tireless proofreading skills that were absolutely necessary to the high quality standards by which this book was published.

To Bob Conradi, who graciously offered his knowledge and opinions to the production and design of this project, as he has so unselfishly for the past three years.

To Dan Poynter, who provided his publishing expertise, both written and verbal, smoothing the rough corners that are inherent to an endeavor of this scope.

To Lee Rohlf, a talented artist, for sticking with us through seemingly impossible demands and deadlines.

To Eric Wulff, a young artist, whose potential is reflected in the illustrations contained on these pages.

To our families and friends, who by their unconditional love and friendship supply constant motivation to seek the highest level in everything we do.

And finally, thanks to the behind-the-scenes cast of experts and professionals who supported us, including: Shawn Scott, Ray Kersting, Allen Fishman, T.J. Romano, Robin Sayre, Frank Riccardo, LaDoris Houston-Payne, Charlotte Britto, Rebecca Ewing, Rob Cunningham, Hattie Hill-Storks, Marion Maxey, John Nash, George Walther, Lori Korn, Art Sobczak, Bob Ratliffe, Gay Denny, Susan Johnston, Daisy Ottman, Allen Feldman, Susan Hill-Wenger, Kathy Stevens, Phyllis Katz, Sharon Krist, Kathy Malloy, Daniel Lukin, and everyone who will read this book, determined to consistently making positive impressions!

Contents

Note to the Reader

Masculine pronouns and possessives are used throughout this book to simplify communication, but the information is of equal value to men and women.

Foreword

In 1988, I was just starting my own free-lance writing company and ran into a former business associate. He was doing telemarketing consulting work for several organizations in the St. Louis area. I had first met Tony Hitt two years prior and had found him to be a charismatic entrepreneur who seemed to motivate people better than anyone I had ever witnessed.

I enjoyed having lunch with him that day and listening to his seemingly endless stream of ideas -- coupled with an energy level to match. As I discussed my new venture with him, I saw a glimmer flash in his eyes, as if yet another light bulb had clicked on in his head. His eyebrows raised as he interrupted me in mid-sentence.

"Did you ever think of writing a book?"

"Of course, I have," I explained. "I'm a writer!" But trying to get my own business off the ground took up most of my waking hours. This particular goal had to wait.

"I don't think so," he continued. "Why don't you help me write a 'phone skills' book?"

Did I forget to mention he was a good salesman? He persuaded me to begin working with him on a book to be titled, *"Positive Impressions."* It would be produced in conjunction with a national seminar of the same name, targeting front-line phone professionals and customer service reps. The following weekend I started organizing his research and piecing it together with information gathered in interviews conducted with Tony on his experiences in the telecommunications field.

At the age of 19, he was already well on his way to becoming a business phone expert. He was hired by one of the country's largest home improvement companies to oversee their national telemarketing offices. At the time he left the position, just two years later, he was responsible for over 2,600 employees in 83 cities.

Upon leaving, he started his own telephone consulting business with clients that included his old employer. With his on-site work, he additionally began speaking to various groups on the importance of the phone as a tool for profit for companies of all sizes. The development of a seminar became the next logical step.

Our goal was to write a book that would be the most comprehensive of its kind. It would include numerous points not included in the time constraints of the seminar. It would also have to be written in the light, practical style that characterizes a reference resource used by busy professionals. Though our foundation was solid, the timing proved faulty. In only a few weeks the project was put on indefinite hold. With the demands from our respective businesses still taking up much of our time, we both felt we were doing an injustice to the material. I packed a box of a dozen or more partial chapters and stored it in my attic.

At the time, I thought little about the future of the book or our initial goals. I also didn't realize that I'd be working for Tony full-time a year later. Now in my fourth year with him, I dusted off that box in my attic just six months ago in September 1991. I'm overwhelmed as I write this "Foreword" and watch this book reach completion.

By any stretch of the imagination, this has not been an easy project. Then again, our goals were extremely ambitious. I can't express the self-satisfaction of completing and publishing a book based on such determination and hard work.

What you are about to read is the compilation of literally thousands of hours of research, organizing, writing, and editing -- the result of years of "in-the-trenches" telephone consulting and observation. In writing, I could not help but learn numerous useful points myself, methods that were immediately adapted to our company telephone policies. Now you have a chance to do the same.

In the three plus years I've worked with Tony, I've gained a priceless education on constantly aiming for peak performance in every area of my life. I consider myself fortunate, not only to have the chance to work with him and learn from him, but to be counted among his friends. My sincere hope is that the presentation of the *"Positive Impressions"* techniques will not only make your job easier, but compel you to be your best everyday.

Read, learn, and think about each chapter and how it relates to your specific job as a telephone pro. Be confident in knowing that you are learning from an experienced trainer and consultant -- Tony Hitt.

May all the impressions you leave with others be positive and productive!

- Kurt Wulff

CHAPTER 1

In the Beginning

The invention of the first practical telephone is credited to Alexander Graham Bell, a professor of vocal physiology at Boston University. Bell set out to develop a telegraph instrument that would send several messages simultaneously over a single wire.

One day, Bell was tuning the springs of the harmonic telegraph receiver by pressing them one by one against his ear, while his assistant Watson, in another room, plucked the transmitter spring to get it vibrating. Surprised by the musical tones set forth by the vibrating, Bell ran into the next room to find that a contact screw on the transmitter was too tight. He discovered that, instead of producing the make-and-break current of a traditional telegraph, the transmitter was producing an uninterrupted flow of current through the circuit. He also realized that what the device could do for one complex sound it could do for all sounds including speech, and gave Watson instructions to build the first telephone based on this principle.

A year later, and after countless experiments with different types of receivers and transmitters, on March 10, 1876, his first complete and understandable sentence was delivered over the line: "Mr. Watson, come here, I want you." Three days earlier the first telephone patent had been issued to Bell.

The first commercial instruments were Bell's "box" type telephones. These were crude, awkward-to-use devices that lacked a good signaling mechanism and required the user to shout into the transmitter. In years to come, improvements in the original telephone design continued to be developed by various individuals, including Thomas Edison. Even so, by 1880 the general nature and theory of operation of most of the components of the modern telephone had been developed.

With the expiration of the original Bell patent in 1894, a multitude of new companies entered the market. Most of these failed or were absorbed by the well-established Bell companies. In 1895, there were nearly 339,000 telephones in use in the United States. As a result of such developments as long-distance transmission, the industry grew by leaps and bounds pushing that figure to 10,475,000 by 1915, to more than 19,602,000 in 1932, and to 40,709,000 in 1950. By 1954, the majority of households had a single black phone that could be used for local or long-distance calls. By the 1960s, companies had turned their concentration to the research of new products and services, those that are popular today.

Today there are more than 130 million access lines in the United States and millions more abroad. According to Alan Feldman, an industry analyst for the Federal Communications Commission (FCC), those lines carried over 402 billion calls in 1991! Most homes have multiple phones in a wide array of colors and styles. Many also have more features than most business phones had available just a few years ago. The business phone can now be computer-driven, with as many features as a company is willing to pay for and program into the system.

So now you know more about the history of the phone than you probably ever wanted to know. Why mention it and where do we go from here?

As the telephone has grown, so has the need for guidelines and superior skills to compete in the marketplace. It used to be that by just having a telephone your company was more progressive or more readily available to provide products and services the consumer wanted. This is no longer the case.

What type of image is your company projecting on the telephone? Whether you are part of a very large organization or work independently, your telephone skills greatly influence people's opinions of your business. It's similar to meeting someone for the first time in person. Each individual quickly draws conclusions about the other by gauging facial expressions, wardrobe, and general demeanor. Unfortunately, on the phone we have only the voice and skills to establish a first impression of another person, but this impression is powerful.

A key concept in advertising is that the consumer's perception is reality. With this in mind, consider each call a mini-advertisement with you as the spokesperson. In only 10 seconds, callers will make solid judgements about you and your company. This is not the time to make mistakes.

If you are beginning to read this book out of duress (for example, the boss said it was a requirement), you'll soon find that it is not such a painful experience and that your supervisor has made at least one good decision recently. If you have picked up the book on your own, I applaud you. You have made the decision to be the best you can be at your job -- the rest of the road will be much easier and fun.

This book is about the superior skills and techniques now needed to effectively compete in an increasingly hostile business environment. It is the "slight edge" that can turn a mediocre organization into the best in its field. We will explore the ways that top telephone professionals use the phone everyday to increase their bottom line profits -- directly and indirectly.

Besides being a person who uses the telephone, you are a consumer. *"Positive Impressions"* is also designed to help you provide your callers with the type of service you expect from the places where you do business.

This book has been written to cover general use of the telephone. To write this book with a single segment in mind (for instance, the medical field) wouldn't be practical. Look at the chapters in this book as a smorgasbord. If you see something you like -- adopt it. If the idea doesn't apply to your situation -- pass. Some of the points might seem like common sense, but these items are often the first forgotten if not practiced on a daily basis. All you might need is a reminder.

Whether you are new to using the telephone in business or have just been assigned new responsibilities involving the phone, or are a seasoned pro, this book will give you powerful new insight. You will increase your command of this "tool of profit" according you the confidence that makes any job fun.

When people attend my seminars, I suggest the following to get the most out of the experience:

Take a plain piece of paper and write "ACTION PLAN" at the top of it. As you read an idea that definitely applies to your situation, make a note that you need to make a change. By the end of the book, you should have a list of several new ways you are going to handle telephone communication. Because it's difficult to change everything at once, prioritize the practices. Take the number one idea and put it into action immediately. When that idea becomes habit, move on to number two, and so forth. Keep your list in a readily visible place where you will be reminded of your commitment daily.

Also, keep your personal copy of this book (with many highlighted areas and notes) close to your work station at all times. You never know when you will be faced with a new telephone responsibility -- collections or prospecting for new business, for instance -- and this book will give you the information that you can begin putting to use. In addition, we have provided a comprehensive Resource Guide in the back of the book. This is a list of sources and publications that were helpful in the research of *"Positive Impressions."* It can serve as an easy reference for those seeking more on specific areas discussed in this book.

Let's get started.

CHAPTER 2

The Caller's Needs

Before we actually get on the telephone, you need to first become better acquainted with your callers. They are just like you and me, and they need your assistance in some way. They might be forced to call you. They might be a product of your expensive advertising campaign or a current customer, helping to make your paycheck possible. A caller could be someone with a product or service that will make your job a little easier or increase business at your company. They might even be a co-worker, associate, or even your boss. Many times in your life, you are a caller. How do you wish to be treated? This brings us to the first rules of effectively handling callers' needs.

The following is a list of the callers' four basic needs:

1. Callers want to be understood. Don't just hear what they say, but listen and understand (see Chapter 11).

2. Callers want to feel welcome and appreciated. Remember, callers are not interruptions in our business. They are the reason for it. Make sure every caller knows you are glad they called -- satisfied or not. If they are calling you, at least they are not calling your competition.

3. Callers want to feel assured. Let your caller know that your company, as well as you personally, are competent and reliable.

This is accomplished both through your words and your actions. At that particular moment, you are a direct reflection of your company to the caller.

4. Callers want to feel special and important. Satisfy the caller by making them feel like they are getting extraordinary service. People like doing business with people that treat them "better." Don't you prefer to go where the clerks seem to give you "extra" attention? Of course you do! (Where everybody knows your name -- like the bar on the television show *"Cheers."*)

Recently, a *USA Today* poll printed the following results: Customers stop doing business with companies for the following reasons:

1%	Died
3%	Moved away
5%	Friends or relatives owned or worked for the competition
9%	Found a better price
14%	Advertising convinced them that another product/brand was better
68%	Perceived an attitude of indifference

That means that nearly 70% of the customers who stopped doing business with a company did so because they didn't think the company really cared about them. As a telephone professional, you are often the most important contact for the caller. You have to do everything in your power to let them know you do care.

This book will assist you in doing that over the telephone. After a thorough read, you will find that most of the points made will easily transfer to face-to-face situations as well.

CHAPTER 3

The Importance of PMA

Attitude is the single most important aspect of any job. It's defined as your mental position with regard to the facts, or in simpler terms, the way you view things. The same principles apply to effective telephone skills. There are five important points to remember about your attitude:

1. Your attitude is what determines your level of job satisfaction, not the hours worked or even your salary.

2. Attitudes are never set in stone. They can always change with a little effort. The choice is yours.

3. Your attitude affects everyone who comes in contact with you. If you come in smiling and ready to do a great job, you will be surprised how fast this can transfer to other people who work with you.

4. Attitude influences behavior. We tend to act the way we feel. It is difficult to hide any type of emotion. Life doesn't deal with us fairly. Sometimes we are going to come into work in a bad mood. This mood, if not kept in check, can have a detrimental effect on our phone communications.

5. Attitudes you transmit you also receive. If you're perceived to be negative or hostile by someone, these feelings will most likely be reflected back to you.

Make a concerted effort to come to work each day with a Positive Mental Attitude (PMA). PMA is a state of mind influenced by your feelings, thoughts, and actions. It's your perception of your job and everything that affects you. Sure, you are going to have bad days just like everyone else. It's the way you react to these situations that separates the pros from the amateurs.

You have probably had days that begin with you feeling great. As the day goes by, however, those good feelings start to fade. By day's end, you are glad it's finally over.

This is something everyone goes through, but even on the worst days, you have some control. Your control begins when you decide that you are responsible for the attitude you display. When you decide to be positive and customer-oriented, you have taken the first step.

For example, suppose your first telephone contact of the day is with an angry customer. This provides you with a choice. You can allow this tough situation to negatively impact your attitude for the rest of the day, or you can put the incident behind you and consciously regain a positive attitude.

Here are a few helpful hints to help you establish and maintain PMA:

1. Start each day with thoughts about the positive aspects of your job.

2. When negative events occur, take a deep breath and re-establish a positive attitude by focusing on activities that allow you to regain your perspective.

3. Whenever possible, avoid people and situations that are predictably negative.

4. Share your attitude when things are going well. Attitudes are caught, not taught.

CHAPTER 4

The "C" Factors

As a telephone professional, you care about giving the best impression every time you pick up the phone. The "C" Factors establish characteristics that are essential in your job and in life. Never lose sight of each one's importance.

1. Caring. This means sincere caring and concern toward the caller, your organization, and yourself. You are not always able to give callers what they want, but you can still convey an "I care" attitude. As for your organization, while conveying this attitude is important, avoid saying anything negative about your company.

Lastly, if you don't care about yourself, there is no way to care for anything or anyone else. Learn to respect yourself and the importance of your job as a telephone professional.

2. Confidence. When you are confident, the caller knows you have the ability to handle his or her needs. Confidence is made up of two parts: technical and interpersonal. Each aspect involves the accumulation of knowledge and experience. The technical end is knowing all the technical aspects of your phone and knowing how to best use each. Do you know the fastest and easiest way to handle each operation of your phone system? It might be a case of simply referring to the manual. If one is not available, ask someone who has more experience with the equipment.

The interpersonal side involves the handling of various situations that inevitably arise on the phone, each of which we will review in following chapters.

3. Consideration. Be considerate of the caller's feelings at all times. Even if you disagree, always try to understand the caller's point of view. Also, try this within your office around your co-workers.

4. Commitment. If you don't know something, take the responsibility to find out as soon as possible. Commit yourself to the caller's satisfaction. Commit yourself to being the best.

5. Creativity. Not many people consider answering the phone a very creative position. I disagree. Think what would happen if you were not creative. When was the last time you said someone was out of the office only to have that person standing right in front of you deciding to take the call? "Hold on. He just walked in." Yeah, right. Without a more creative approach, you stand the chance of looking foolish and irritating the caller. Also, most workers have other responsibilities besides answering the telephone. It takes a great amount of creativity to answer three lines at the same time you are giving two salesmen their messages, typing a letter for the boss, filing, running the copier . . . Well, you get the idea. Your job not only needs creativity, it demands it!

6. Control. You must display the discipline needed to control your emotions, whatever the situation. There is no question that angry callers can get out of hand, but never take their verbal assaults personally. Most importantly, never return their fire. Rarely are these comments directed toward you specifically and you can only hurt yourself by retaliating. A retailer's adage states, "The customer is always right." I do not believe this is always true. I believe the customer is always the customer. With this, the customer has certain rights, but there are still boundaries.

7. Contagious. I'm not talking about a potential health hazard.

I'm talking about a combination of enthusiasm and Positive Mental Attitude that rubs off on every caller and those who work around you.

8. Communication. As a telephone professional, you are the center of communication for your company. Often you are the first person to sense a problem. Make a determined effort to communicate these situations to the appropriate people. Follow up. Find out what actions were taken to solve the problem. For instance, what if a customer reports to you that they continue to call everyday, but your boss has not returned the individual's call for over a week? You might approach your boss and see if there is any way you can help or possibly even return the call for him.

CHAPTER 5

Voice & Personality

One of the most important tools you have on the telephone is your voice. "Obviously," you say. Obvious maybe, but when was the last time you analyzed your "voice personality?" Or how about those who work around you? Communications experts agree that the elements and characteristics surrounding the words (such as tone of voice, inflections, or facial expressions) make up over 90% of the communicated message. The definitions of the actual words make up less than 10% of what is communicated to the receiver!

It is impossible to overstate the importance of using your voice as an asset on the telephone. When you are face-to-face many elements other than the voice come into play -- facial expressions, body movements, eye direction, etc. On the phone, your voice alone dictates every message you want to send, or do not wish to deliver, to the receiver. There are very few second chances.

To start, here are five points that form the basis of an effective voice personality:

1. Be alert. Give the impression you are wide-awake, alert, and interested in the person calling.

2. Sound pleasant (in other words -- be in a good mood). Speak in a "voice with a smile." A smile in your voice can perform magic. Those who call don't have the opportunity to be won over with your facial expressions -- they only have your voice to judge you and your company. Now get to work putting the smile into your everyday work habits on the phone!

3. **Be natural.** Speak as straightforwardly as possible. Avoid technical language or industry jargon that could alienate those individuals who might not be experts in your field.

4. **Speak clearly and concisely.** Get to the point quickly, but understandably. Do not be afraid to open your mouth wide. When you don't, you risk mumbling.

5. **Expressiveness.** Don't be afraid to fill your voice, and your tone, with expression. This does not mean yelling into the phone. We will talk a little later about the best way to vary the pitch and inflection of your voice.

There are also physical attributes to your voice personality. With the correct training, each can be used to deliver the speaking quality you need to confidently handle any caller as a telephone professional.

Breathing

I think that you will agree that everyone knows how to breathe. This simple fact of nature is the most important factor in what we call "voice exercises."

Why would you want to exercise your voice? Well, most of us are not born with the best speaking voices. Just as a great athlete must work to keep his muscles firm and flexible, the same can be done with the voice, fortunately, with a lot less effort than the athlete has to put into his sport.

Actors, singers, and other public personalities work diligently on improving their voices and breathing. For anyone who uses his or her voice on the phone to generate or manage business, the importance of your breathing is no less important. By breathing deeply from the diaphragm you are able to complete a sentence without stopping to catch your breath.

To understand the difference, place this book on the ground and read from it as you bend toward it while remaining seated. Your words will naturally be coming from the diaphragm. As you resume the upright position, continue reading in the same way and you will have valuable feedback on the results you should experience from diaphragm speech.

Articulation

The three parts of your face that must move in order to speak clearly are the lips, tongue, and jaw. To realize their collective effect on the articulation of your words, try this exercise. Try saying your name and the name of your company aloud, without moving your lips, jaw, or tongue. Then say these words with the proper movements.

As you can see, in order to move the lips, tongue, and jaw freely and speak articulately, you cannot have a mouthful of gum or a cigarette dangling from your lips. Although telephone equipment has come a long way since the early days, even the most sensitive equipment cannot make up for poor pronunciation. Anyway, the last thing your company wants is someone popping bubbles while in a phone conversation with a potential client.

To ensure that you are presenting a clear message over the telephone, practice whispering the words that you might say when talking to a caller. When you whisper, you are forced to open your mouth wider than normal and use your lips more to pronunciate. When you return to your normal volume, use the same techniques as when you are whispering.

For additional practice, if you have young children at home, you might have the perfect articulation resource guide at your fingertips. Dr. Seuss books read aloud are helpful in making the reader pronounce every word clearly.

Try these other "articulation" exercises on the following pages:

THE NUMBERS GAME

Careful pronunciation and inflection are necessary when giving telephone numbers and dollar amounts. Some numbers may sound alike over the telephone -- and misunderstandings can be costly! Practice this list:

Number	Pronunciation	Formation of Sound
0	OH	Long O
1	WuN	Strong W and N
2	Too	Strong T and Long OO
3	th-R-ee	Strong R and Long EE
4	Fo-eR	Long O and Strong R
5	fi-iV	First I Long, Second I Short, Strong V
6	SiKS	Strong S and KS
7	SeV-en	Strong S and V, Well-rounded EN
8	aTe	Long A and Strong T
9	Ni-eN	First N Strong, Long I, Mild Emphasis on EN

THE VOWELS GAME

Vowels	Sounded as in:	Position of Mouth
A	Father	open
A	Ate	half open
A	Call	open, lips slightly round
A	Hat	half open
E	He	almost closed
E	Met	slightly open
I	Kite	open, then closing
I	It	slightly open
O	Hot	open
O	Old	open, lips rounded
U	Flute	almost closed, lips round
U	Hut	half open
OI	Oil	open, then closing
OU	South	open, then closing

Inflection

Inflection adds enthusiasm, alertness, and color to your voice, and avoids a boring monotone. The human voice is capable of hundreds of inflections. The Chinese have based much of the meaning of their language on the emphasis placed on the sounds in each of their words. For example, the word "yen" has four completely different meanings -- each defined only in the way they are spoken.

The use of inflection in the English language is also essential to effectively communicating. The mood of a sentence can be changed drastically merely be accentuating a certain syllable. "Good-BYE," for example, implies that you hope you never talk to that person again!

It's also possible to stress the importance of a particular word simply by saying it at a higher pitch.

"It is SO nice to hear from you, Mr. Smith!"

By emphasizing the word "so" your remark becomes friendlier and more enthusiastic. The caller cannot help but be open to what you will say after such a greeting. Of course, it is up to you, depending on the particular situation, to decide which words to emphasize. No matter what you choose, always try to put some variations in your speech.

Sometimes a slight hesitation or pause can make the biggest difference. In business, it's generally helpful to pause slightly after the receiver's name. For instance:

"Of course, Mr. Braddock . . . Mr. Kersting will be HAPPY to see you tomorrow."

At the same time, a pause after the name of your product can also set up a powerful mental picture in the mind's eye of the customer on the other end of the line.

"Yes, Mr. Braddock . . . POSITIVE IMPRESSIONS . . . is a fine

book to teach all of your employees effective phone skills." (excuse the blatant plug)

At first you will need to put some serious practice into special uses of inflection, but after a few weeks you will find it will come naturally. As you practice, remember -- although variations in the volume of your voice are important -- don't take it too far. Speaking too loudly into the phone will irritate some callers. It can blur your speech such as those usually heard emanating from a fast food, drive-through speaker. The secret is to speak in a normal tone, with a variety of inflections, but with little change in volume (Best Indicator: No matter what your points of inflection are, the volume of your voice should be such that a person standing two paces behind you cannot understand what you are saying).

Rate of Speech

A distinct, moderate rate of speech saves repetition and prevents potentially harmful misunderstandings. If a person is rushed, he or she soon gives up and makes no effort to understand. Hurried speech can be slurred. Take the time to enunciate every word clearly, or you will speak too quickly. On the other hand, speaking too slowly causes thoughts to sound disjointed and lose their meaning. This may also tend to give the impression of being unsure of your statements. Uncertainty is not a quality that generates more dollars for any company.

Voice Pitch

Your voice doesn't sound the same to you as it does to others. You hear your voice as it echoes throughout the bone structure of your head. This muffles many of the higher tones, making it sound much lower than it really is.

It's critical that your voice is superb! Your voice and the way you sound is just as important to you as it is to radio personalities. D.J.'s are constantly listening to tapes of their voices and making changes. You should do the same.

Try listening to a tape recording of your voice. "Do I really sound like that?" is a common reaction of many people. The answer is "yes." For the most part that is exactly how you sound to other people. Record your voice at various times of the day in 15-minute intervals. Play back the tape and listen carefully to your voice. If you were the person on the other end of the line, how would you perceive yourself and the company? You will find that your voice will vary at different times of the day. For instance, as a general rule people sound better in the morning. Repeat the test every three months to ensure a consistent, pleasant voice pitch on the telephone.

Many people also have higher-pitched voices. With a few minutes practice a day, this can be changed over time. Once a day, take five minutes to hum in a lower than normal key. The method also works in reverse for those with deep, monotone voices. This is one of the methods used successfully by opera coaches -- past and present.

Avoid the trap of raising the pitch of your voice when talking on the telephone. This generally happens when individuals are upset, excited, or nervous. With practice, you will speak in a normal, natural pitch that will be pleasant, and even comforting, to those on the other end of the line.

CHAPTER 6

Smile!

"Smile and the world smiles back at you."

No telephone book is complete without a few words on smiling. Since I started studying telephone communications, everything I read, heard, or watched mentions the importance of a big smile.

A smile, or lack thereof, can be detected. A smile always makes you feel better. Even if you have to initially force your smile, it eventually -- and almost immediately -- makes you feel better.

Smiling relieves stress. Smiles are contagious. It's difficult to be mad at someone who is happy and smiling. In addition to bettering your attitude toward others, and others toward you, it helps in other ways. A smile is actually physically easier than a frown. It's easier to enunciate when you are smiling. Therefore, when you are smiling others can better understand what you are saying (Since the smile is contagious, then the other person will smile and also be easier to understand).

Place a mirror in easy access to your work station. When you pick up the telephone give it a glance to make sure your smile is intact. Some phone pros actually place "smiling" faces and/or smile signs to remind them of the importance of a BIG SMILE! In telemarketing training manuals, I've often seen the catchy phrase "Smile and Dial."

I support whatever it takes to make smiling on the job a habit.

Smile for others, smile for yourself, smile to be better understood.

Smile!

CHAPTER 7

Basic Manners

Why a chapter on basic manners? This is common sense. Well, maybe, but it never hurts to review manners in any situation.

1. **The words "please" and "thank you" always go a long way when it comes to making a caller feel welcome and appreciated.** Never miss an opportunity to make any caller feel special.

2. **Don't talk (or listen) and eat, drink, chew gum, or smoke at the same time.** It is rude in person, and it is rude on the phone. The caller can hear you smacking gum or blowing smoke. Even if he could not hear you, you should be devoting 100% of your attention to the caller.

3. **Don't talk to someone around you during a phone conversation.** If it is absolutely necessary, excuse yourself and politely place the caller on hold, if the caller approves. Simply covering the receiver is never acceptable and leaves you open for a very embarrassing situation.

4. **Always excuse yourself after sneezing or coughing on the phone.** Just like Mom told you!

CHAPTER 8

Developing Rapport

The ability to develop rapport, or trust, is important in almost all types of communication. Whether a business telephone call or casual conversation with a department store clerk, there is no better way to quickly gain valuable information and personal credibility. In business specifically, the more callers that feel comfortable with you and the company (you are the company to them), the more you are positioned to sell, or at the very least, to handle their needs. It's always easier to talk to a friend!

Because of this, the art of developing rapport with customers and employees is one of the core characteristics found in most successful business leaders. They are trusted. Fortunately, the skills needed to improve your abilities in this area are not exclusive to a select group of top corporate officers.

For instance, "listening." Do you know how to listen? Most people are sure that they know how to listen and have no problems with it, particularly on the telephone. I have news for you: It isn't true! In business alone, millions of real and potential earnings are lost to poor listening habits everyday. By improving your listening habits you will not only go a long way in developing rapport, but you will quickly gain control of the phone call.

Though important, listening certainly isn't the only ingredient to successfully developing rapport. As opportunities arise, use the five following techniques to further develop rapport in any type of situation. They are not difficult, but too many people fail to put the concepts into everyday practice. Your ability to turn these points into habit will already put you heads above 90% of your competition.

1. Get and use the other person's name. The famous American educator Dale Carnegie had a saying: "The sweetest sound to any person is the sound of his own name." People love to hear their name said aloud. What can you do if you don't know the other person's name? As with anything, often the easiest way to obtain something is to ask. Many times you can directly ask "What is your name?" without any problem. A more comfortable method for others is called the sharing method. For instance, "My name is Tony. What is yours?"

There is also the fill-in-the-blank method. "And your name is _______?" This particular approach should be used sparingly because it can easily be perceived as underhanded.

Particularly in telephone conversations, always avoid such obvious tricks as "How did you spell that last name again?" when it's obvious the name has never been spoken. You might get an embarrassing response such as "That's J-O-N-E-S." With only a few words, your credibility could be permanently damaged. Don't risk it.

2. Find common ground. People tend to trust those individuals with whom they have found the most in common. From the outset of the conversation, it must be apparent to the other person that your aims are the same as his or hers. Without making things up, grasp onto an area of interest with the person and link it to your own life. "You just got back from Florida? I've always wanted to go there." Without being a phony expert on the Sunshine State, you will successfully link with the individual's world.

Another method is to find a common link through "mirroring" (see Chapter 10). This includes speaking faster if you are conversing with a fast-talker or speaking softer if the person appears more shy or introverted. Some telemarketing experts go so far as to change their dialects to reflect those of the caller.

3. Ask questions about the other person's viewpoint. Ask lots of questions, but be smart. This is where knowing your company and the services you provide is important. When handling a complaint or trying to sell someone, respond positively to each of the customer's comments. Even if you don't agree, answer with, "I understand where you are coming from on that issue."

People always prefer to work with someone who is interested in what they think.

4. Know the desired result of the communication. You cannot get from point A to point B unless you know where they are located. Know the objective of the communication. If you are trying to make a sale, the objective might be to supply the customer with a satisfying product at a reasonable price. If you are handling a complaint, the outcome should be to quickly and effectively resolve the conflict. Make certain both parties are consistently on target by restating your objective when needed and probing for further details throughout the conversation. Hidden agendas can ruin rapport.

5. Be flexible. Always be willing to bend. Any relationship, whether business or personal, needs to be a series of compromises on both sides. No trust will be gained by either party's inability to budge on an issue. If you initiate a flexible attitude, the other individual will often also become more willing to make compromises.

Use these ideas as guidelines -- not as steadfast laws of communication. Different personalities could make use of all five points difficult in every situation. Without rapport there is no real communication.

CHAPTER 9

Keeping It Positive

Is the glass half full or half empty? The way you view things has a tendency to sway the way you say things. We have already talked about trying to be positive in our lives and on the telephone. The following are some of the most commonly used, or actually misused, words and phrases that create a negative image or impact on callers:

1. "I'll try."
"I'll try to get back with you by the end of the day."

This sounds like you cannot promise anything and, more than likely, nothing will get accomplished. State only what you will do.

Say: "I will call you first thing in the morning."

2. "I'm not sure."
"I'm not sure to whom you should speak about that."

Only mention what you are sure you can deliver. There is no need to deal with vague possibilities.

Say: "One moment, I'll find out who would be the best person with whom you should speak regarding your situation."

3. "I can't; we can't; you can't."
"We can't refund your money."

Nobody cares about what you can't do. Tell them only what can be

done to alleviate the problem.
Say: "I can send you a credit voucher for your next purchase."

4. "I'll be honest with you . . ." or "To tell you the truth..."
"I'll be honest with you, I don't think you'll see anything until tomorrow."

This implies that you were previously being dishonest. Eliminate this entirely from your conversations. Just be honest. Say what you can do, and then do it.
Say: "I will make sure you see the report by tomorrow at 2:00."

5. "You have . . ."
"You have to bring in the defective one."

No, the caller doesn't have to do anything. The magic word is still "please."
Say: "Will you please bring in the defective one so I can give you a replacement -- with our compliments, of course."

6. "You should have . . ." or "Why didn't you . . ."
"You should have called us within 24 hours of delivery of your new furniture."

Pointing the finger never helps anything and proves to be totally unprofessional. This reaction will only make the caller defensive and probably angrier.
Say: "Our truck will be by tomorrow to replace the table top -- with our compliments, of course."

7. "There's nothing I can do."
"There is nothing I can do about the problem, Mr. Perry."

There is always something you can do. List the actions you are able to take. No one wants to hear any negative solutions, particularly after lodging a complaint.
Say: "Mr. Perry, I can connect you with Adam Patrick in our Service Department. He will be able to assist you."

8. "You made a mistake."

"You made a mistake, Ms. Thornburg. That deadline was last Friday."

It just doesn't matter and calling it a mistake doesn't help the situation. Once again, "please" will go a long way in calming any frayed nerves.

Say: "Will you please mail that to me today, Ms. Thornburg. I'll see that it gets to the correct department."

9. "Your complaint."

"I'll tell Mr. Baron about your complaint."

The caller may not even recognize it is a complaint unless you call it that. Try to diminish the seriousness of the situation by calling it a question or comment. The word "complaint" can put the caller in a more aggressive posture.

Say: "I'll pass your comments on to Mr. Baron."

10. "Your problem."

"I'm sure we can handle your problem."

Once again, the connotation of the word is negative. Try substituting the word "situation."

Say: "I'm certain we can handle your situation to your complete satisfaction."

11. "I'm sorry."

"I'm sorry you feel that way."

Most of the time when I hear "I'm sorry" on the telephone it sounds about as sincere as "Have a nice day" does at the grocery store checkout counter. Try empathizing instead.

Say: "I can understand how you feel."

12. "I hope. . ." or "This should. . ."

"This should solve your problem."

Both of these phrases convey doubt or uncertainty. Always be definite when resolving a problem.

Say: "This will remedy your situation."

13. "I'm just . . ."
"I'm just calling to see if you received the information I mailed."
"I'm just his assistant . . ."

Your job and your actions in business are important and you should in no way diminish their value with these types of statements. Say: "I'm calling today to confirm . . ." or "I'm his assistant. I'll get the information for you."

Ever since I have been speaking on communications skills, I have centered most of my attention on these 13 words and phrases. I am constantly receiving notes from past seminar participants and acquaintances to add to my list. I have always thought eventually I would put them together in a feature article, or even a book. George Walther beat me to the punch.

Earlier this year, Putnam published Walther's *"Power Talking: 50 Ways to Say What You Mean and Get What You Want."* This book elaborates on the points I have mentioned and many others. If you are serious about becoming a more effective communicator on the telephone and in all areas of your job, I highly recommend the book (see Resource Guide for more information).

CHAPTER 10

Mirroring the Caller's Style

One key to establishing rapport is finding "common ground." This enables you to appear more familiar to the caller -- their feelings and their needs. Human nature attracts us to people with whom we share common ideas, feelings, and interests.

Though there are several ways to establish common ground with callers, the technique of "mirroring" is very popular. Mirroring is the act of reflecting the personality traits of the caller. It means slowing or increasing your rate of speech to reflect that of the caller. The practice can be used with equal success in both sales and customer service phone use.

To use a common example, if you are talking to someone from the deep South, you might find that this individual speaks slower than what you generally hear. You would then slow your speech to more closely match that of the other party. On the other hand, a resident of the Northeast, such as New York City, might be accustomed to a much quicker pace represented by their faster pattern of speech.

Some telephone professionals I have spoken with take it so far as to change their own accents to reflect various regional differences. I know of one telemarketing firm based in Chicago and located at the top of one of the city's largest skyscrapers. Many of their calls are placed to "small town" America. They have found that in these situations the prospects are much more comfortable speaking to a pitchman with a "good ole boy" accent instead of the big city telephone salespeople. As far as they are concerned, the big city people talk too fast and are perceived to be distrustful. The perception is reality -- particularly on the telephone.

NOTE: If you don't do accents well, don't do accents.

Another form of mirroring focuses on the way each of us uses our senses. Each of us takes in information through our sight (visual), our hearing (auditory), and through what we feel (kinesthetic). Although everyone uses all three, one is generally dominant. By listening carefully to the phrases the caller uses, you can tell which sense best describes the person and then begin mirroring it in your own speech.

1. Visual

These individuals prefer to speak face-to-face rather than talk on the phone. They will usually speak more quickly than the average caller and with a higher tone. They focus on how things look, instead of how they feel about an idea. Listen for phrases that are visually-oriented such as:

- Do you get the picture?
- It appears . . .
- I foresee. . .
- I'm getting a clear mental picture.
- I see what you mean.

2. Auditory

These people enjoy hearing themselves talk. They enjoy talking on the telephone as much as anything they do. Loud, annoying sounds tend to irritate them easily so they usually speak in distinctive, comforting tones. They are articulate individuals who analyze the world around them by listening to the sounds. They use phrases related to their dominant sense of hearing such as:

- It doesn't sound reasonable to me.

- Is there a hidden message?
- The noise is distracting me.
- In a manner of speaking.
- I hear what you're saying.
- I don't like the tone of your voice.
- That rings a bell.

3. Kinesthetic

The world around these individuals is based on their feelings at a given moment, or in simpler terms, gut reactions. They often have trouble verbalizing these feelings. A pat on the back to them can be worth a thousand words. Their speech patterns are accompanied by long pauses and a slow, meticulous rate. Listen for phrases such as:

- I feel comfortable about this.
- It shook me up.
- That's so much for me to deal with.
- I had a hunch about . . .
- You're not in touch with . . .

Sometimes it will be more difficult to determine just which one best characterizes a particular caller. In these situations, try using phrases from all three sense groups in your mirroring. You can't go wrong!

CHAPTER 11

Powerful Listening Skills

The vast majority of this book has been dedicated to conveying messages via the telephone. But is listening on the telephone any less important? The answer is an emphatic "No."

S.I. Hayakawa, a well-known semanticist and educator, once noted that listening for most people is "simply maintaining a polite silence while you are rehearsing in your mind the speech you are going to make the next time you can grab a conversational opening." The cost of this type of communication can be devastating, particularly in business. Sperry Corporation points out in one of its advertisements that if each of 100 million workers made one $10 listening mistake, it would cost $1 billion!

The following are some elementary points to listening more effectively in person and on the telephone:

1. Listening is not a matter of intelligence. As a matter of fact, good listening habits are created through experience, good training, and lots of practice. Though people would often like to blame listening mistakes on stupidity, this is rarely the real cause.

2. Good hearing and good listening are not the same. Good hearing doesn't necessarily lead to good listening. It is simply the first step in listening. It's the physical activity involving sound waves striking the eardrum, setting a complex hearing process into action. Listening, on the other hand, is a mental activity.

Comments such as "I often have trouble hearing what people say" and "The room was too noisy" generally refer to outside interferences. Comments such as "I wasn't interested" or "I was thinking about something else" point at mental blocks to effective listening. Each problem is equally important to optimal communication.

3. You never stop training yourself to become a better listener. A successful basketball coach once said, "Practice doesn't make perfect. Practice makes permanent." He meant that if we practice daily doing something the wrong way, we will simply make the wrong way permanent. With no training, we may be practicing listening habits poorly until these poor habits become permanent.

Most of us walk every day. Maybe you enjoy jogging. We have participated in these activities since we were about a year old, yet not many of us expect to become a track star or a marathon runner. We realize that we would need special training to prepare for such an event. Let's consider this same idea in relation to listening. We need to train ourselves a little each day until we become power listeners.

4. Oral Communication is a two-way street. Someone attending one of my seminars told me once, "I could be a great communicator if I could just become a better speaker." Fortunately, the speaker doesn't have 100% of the responsibility. It's a two-way transaction. Listening is as much, if not more, a part of effective communication as the spoken word.

Consider what I call the "25% solution." This means only talking 25% (or one-fourth) of the time. When we allow the other person to talk, we provide an atmosphere where issues can begin to resolve themselves.

5. Listening should be active, not passive. You might believe that listening involves no work or effort on our part. Our ears do the work anyway.

Efficient listening demands a great deal of energy. Imagine

yourself listening to some important sporting event on the radio. You might visualize the field and the positions of the players. You become excited and caught up in the broadcast, hanging passionately onto each of the announcer's comments. You get this excited because you care about who wins. You can get that involved in any listening situation when you choose to become an active listener. This means not only absorbing the words spoken, but also listening for "word pictures." These include an individual's tone of voice and emotions.

6. Concentrate on the main ideas in the message. Everything in a message, whether it comes formally or informally, is centered around a main idea. It is sometimes easy to become sidetracked by the examples or stories people may use to support an idea. Identify the main idea first, rather than use all your listening energy on the supporting details. Additionally, learn to empathize with the caller. If you are able to put yourself in the other person's shoes, you will more easily be able to concentrate on his needs.

7. Offer oral feedback to the speaker. Your feedback as a listener helps the speaker understand the effect of his message on you and allows you to get the real meaning of the message. Try "verbal nods" such as "I understand," "I can see your point," "Go on," "Hmmm, interesting," or a simple "Yes," to let the person know you are listening and to encourage them to continue speaking. If you have ever had the experience where you are on the telephone and the caller asks, "Are you still there?" you probably need to improve your feedback techniques.

8. Consciously formulate questions. When you listen to new information, it's important that you ask both open- and closed-ended questions (see Chapter 12) to make sure you understand what the speaker is trying to say. If anything that was said is unclear to you, you can ask immediately to have it repeated or explained. You can also paraphrase what the speaker has said to determine if you comprehend the message correctly. Your goal is to have no loose ends when the conversation is over.

9. Avoid judgment. Most of us have a natural tendency to pass judgment on the world around us. This is not an attribute that will help anyone as a telephone professional. Don't allow your feelings to influence your perception of the caller's message. Respond to the issues, not the individual. Don't let yourself be irritated or distracted by things the caller says or the way they are said. For example, if a caller is angry and shouting on the phone, listen for the root of the problem, not how loudly he is yelling.

10. Let them finish. Not only is it an effective listening habit, but it's just good manners. Don't interrupt or put words in the caller's mouth. Let them complete the entire story and then ask questions. Usually when you interrupt, the individual starts the story over again. Save yourself the time and aggravation.

11. Take notes at every stage. Doing so will crystallize what you and the speaker are saying and also will give you an accurate reference point if you need to pass the information to another person in your office or refer back to the facts in the future. While you are writing, let the caller know you are doing so. This indicates to them that what they are saying is truly important to you.

Never assume anything. Assumptions will make an ASS out of U and ME. Accurate information is the best approach.

CHAPTER 12

Asking the Right Questions

Being able to accurately collect all of the information initially will save you time and reduce your possibilities for misunderstandings. This is particularly true in customer service positions where you hear details describing a complaint or a problem. A combination of open- and closed-ended questions is the best method to satisfy the needs of both the customer and your own company.

Open-ended Questions

These are questions that cannot be answered with a simple "yes" or "no" response. Each of your questions should start with one of the journalists' best friends: who, what, when, where, why, how.

For example:

Who? With whom did you speak ? Who are you?

What? What happened? What do you want to happen?

When? When did it happen? When should it be sent?

Where? Where is it now? Where should it go?

Why? Why did it happen? (This assures the incident will not be repeated.)

How? How can we resolve this situation?

By using each of these six words, you will easily be able to determine each of the caller's needs. In addition, use his name to lead off each question. You will be able to grab his attention before getting to the actual question. Then, by asking specifically for his opinions or ideas, chances are they will answer in greater detail. Personalize your questions like:

"Bob, tell me how you'd react to . . ."

"Joanne, I'd like your opinion on . . ."

"Mr. Simpson, let me know your personal feelings about . . ."

"Ms. Byington, what are your thoughts on . . ."

It doesn't end there. Before you hang up you need to verify the information you wrote down (You did remember to write everything down?) after each of the questions. This is best done with closed-ended questions.

Closed-ended Questions

Closed-ended questions can be answered with a simple "yes" or "no." They are best used to confirm understanding by both you and the caller. Sometimes, as hard as you or the caller might try, you cannot get on the same wavelength. If you were to act on only part of the issue, you could add another unnecessary problem.

After the caller answers your initial open-ended line of questioning, confirm each piece of information on your list. For example:

"You'll be available for a return call after 2:00?"

"Yes."

If you misunderstood or wrote down an incorrect point, you will immediately know.

CHAPTER 13

Knowing Your Telephone System

You can never master the skills needed to be a complete telephone professional without fully knowing your phone system. Today, take it upon yourself to become the office expert. Be the one whom anyone can ask whenever they are unsure how to handle a particular operation of your company's phone system. Who better than you, the person handling the majority of the calls, to be the resident master of every feature of the telephone.

Need more reasons? In your position, no matter if you are a customer service rep or a receptionist, one wrong transfer or inadvertent disconnect and the perceived competence level of you and your company dramatically drops. Why risk this loss in potential revenue and image by not adequately understanding the tool of your trade -- the telephone.

Lori Korn, a training consultant with CalTel Communications in Glendale, California, provides an approach for the new employee trying to learn an unfamiliar phone system.

Let's say you just started a new job. You probably got an orientation where they reviewed such things as employee benefits, company procedures, vacation policies, and other related topics. Now sitting at your new desk you notice a sophisticated looking telephone covered with rows of feature buttons. How do you find out how to use it? Can you perform your job effectively if you don't know how to use your telephone? Your first course of action should be to search out the resources that are immediately available.

• **Ask your co-workers.** While they probably do not know all the bells-and-whistles features, they probably do know the basic telephone operations.

• **Determine if your company offers any telephone training.** Many companies offer a telephone training session to new employees. Many new employees are inclined to skip it, thinking it's not important. Wrong assumption! If your company offers such training, take advantage of it -- it can be a lifesaver.

• **See if there is an available user's guide.** These guides or manuals are generally published by the telephone system manufacturer. They can explain the phone's features and operations. However, be certain to use this type of guide carefully. It may contain features or operations for which your particular telephone or system may not be programmed.

• **Check to see if your company has a customized user guide and directory that relates specifically to the way your system is configured.**

• **See if the telephone system manufacturer has an available videotape which explains the telephone operation.** Better yet, suggest that your company videotape one of the new employee telephone orientations, which would naturally be more customized to your company's applications.

Once you gather available resources you may be shocked by the sheer number of techniques available through the proper use of your phone. Do not be overwhelmed. You do not have to learn them all at once. In the beginning, concentrate only on those features that are essential to performing your job. Some essential features include:

1. Transfer. How do you transfer a call to another extension? This function is usually performed by pressing the TRANSFER button, dialing the extension number, announcing the call and hanging up.

Some systems may require you to press the TRANSFER once more before hanging up to complete the transfer. What else might you want to know about transferring calls?

• What happens to a transferred call if it is not answered? Will it return to you? To the operator? Can you get it back?

• Is there a different procedure for transferring unscreened (when you don't wait to announce the call) versus screened (when you announce the transfer first)? Can you turn a screened transfer into a conference call? How?

2. Hold. Using the HOLD button is something most people can handle, but what should you know about the hold feature?

• Can you retrieve a hold call from any station, or only from the telephone instrument where the call is holding?

• Will a call on hold stay on hold forever, or will it ring back after a certain period of time? If so, how long? What happens if you don't answer the call after it rings back? Does it return to the operator?

• Does your system offer exclusive hold? This restricts someone else from accidently picking up a call holding for you.

3. Pick-up. Call pick-up is a feature used to answer other ringing phones. Group pick-up is often programmed to allow anyone within a department to answer any ringing phone in the group, even if they don't know the extension of the ringing phone, generally by pressing a PICK-UP key. This feature allows easier coverage of departmental phones without the necessity of physically going over to the ringing instrument. What should you find out about pick-up?

• Which phones are in your pick-up group?

• What happens if two or more phones are ringing at once?

• Can you pick up a particular ringing line if more than one is ringing (often called "Directed Call Pick-up")?

4. Placing Calls. How do you call out? Do you dial 9 for all calls? Most systems today are programmed so that when you dial 9, the telephone system will choose the most economical route, select a line for you, and send the call -- but check. Some companies have complex networks where it might be necessary to dial all kinds of access codes to reach other company locations or long distance destinations.

5. Call Coverage. What happens to your call if you are not available to answer it? Does it return to the operator or forward to a secretary, message center, or voice mail? If so, under what conditions? When your line is busy? After four rings? Find out how your telephone line is configured and what your options are for coverage.

6. Call Waiting. How do you know that there is another call coming in for you when you are already on a call? Do you have a second line key on your telephone? Do you get a call waiting indication? If so, how do you place your first call on hold to answer the second?

Knowing these basics will give you an understanding of most office telephones. There are many other features that, while not crucial for day-to-day functioning, can make your work easier or more productive. Check into these features and operations as well:

• **Callback.** The callback feature is used to reach someone within your company whose line is frequently busy. It can be an extremely useful feature when you have difficulty reaching an individual.

If you call an internal party and hear a busy signal, you would usually depress your CALLBACK key and hang up. When the called party is free, your telephone will ring (usually with a distinctive ring) and your CALLBACK key will probably flash. When you answer the call back ring, the other party will immediately be rung.

• **Call Forward.** The call forward feature allows you to redirect your calls to another station, usually by pressing the FORWARD button and dialing the extension number where you want your calls redirected. Some systems may require you to press the FORWARD button again to complete the feature set-up. Often, the FORWARD key will light or flash to remind you that your calls are being re-routed. What else should you know about call forwarding?

Does the system forward your calls immediately, or after a certain number of rings? Can you forward to the operator (usually "yes") or directly to your voice mailbox (sometimes -- you'll need to check)? Does the system automatically forward your calls (see "Call Coverage" section in this chapter), or do you have to manually initiate this action? Can internal calls be routed differently than external callers? Can your secretary override your forwarding to route screened calls to you? How does your system remind you that your calls are forwarded?

• **Conference.** Conference calling allows you to add parties into an established call. It's usually accomplished, with the first party already on the line, by pressing the CONFERENCE key, dialing the next party, waiting for an answer, and re-depressing the CONFERENCE key. Here are a few other items to look for in your research:

How many parties can be in the conference call (systems vary from 3 to 8)? How about the mix of outside versus internal parties (many phone systems allow only two outside parties, but a larger number of internal ones)? What happens if the originator or any participant drops out of the call? Will the others be disconnected?

When two people are on hold while an additional party is being added to the conference, can they talk to each other? How do you drop someone from the conference?

• **Last Number Redial.** Most phone systems automatically store the last number you dial. It can usually be redialed by simply pressing a REDIAL button on your telephone. Check to see if your system stores all dialed numbers or just outside numbers.

• **Message Notification.** How do you know that you have messages waiting for you? Many telephone systems have a MESSAGE key that will either light or flash when you do. The MESSAGE key can be lit by either the attendant, a message center operator, your voice mailbox, or sometimes by another user. On most systems, simply pressing your MESSAGE key will ring you back to the party who is holding your messages.

If you have a single line telephone or don't have a MESSAGE key, your telephone system may use a stutter or broken dial tone to indicate that you have messages. To retrieve them, dial the extension number of the message center.

• **Night Answer.** How are your company's calls handled after hours when the switchboard is closed? Many companies route calls to a night chime so that employees working late can answer the calls from any telephone. If your company uses night answer and you work late, check to see how to pick up calls from the night bell. This is usually accomplished by dialing an access code or by depressing a NIGHT key on your telephone set.

• **Page.** Check to see if your company has a paging system. See if pages must go through the attendant, or if anyone can page. Paging from a telephone set is usually done by pressing the PAGE key or by dialing an access code. You may want to see if paged announcements go through ceiling speakers, telephone speaker phones, or both, and see which areas of your offices can clearly hear the pages.

• **Speaker phone.** A speaker phone can be a wonderful tool if used appropriately. You should find out:

How to originate a call on speaker (usually by pressing the SPEAKER button while the phone is on hook). How you move a call from the handset to the speaker (usually by pressing and holding the SPEAKER button and placing the handset in the cradle). How you take a call off speaker (usually by simply lifting the handset). Can your telephone receive voice announcements from secretaries and co-workers? This feature allows internal calls to come through your speaker, and generally allows you to answer back without touching your telephone. Can you originate voice announced calls to others?

• **Mute.** The MUTE button allows you to speak freely without a caller hearing. While the key is depressed you can still hear the caller, but they cannot hear anything on your end. Do not get into a habit of covering the mouthpiece end of the telephone as a substitute for the MUTE or HOLD buttons. Telephones are now produced with microphones in both ends of the receiver -- including the earpiece that you probably will not cover with your hand. The caller will still be able to faintly hear what you are saying. I have been in enough offices, and heard enough things, to know this isn't a good idea.

• **Speed Dialing.** Speed dialing comes in two varieties. System speed dial provides a company-wide list of numbers that can be accessed from any telephone, generally by pressing a SYSTEM SPEED or STATION SPEED key followed by a two- or three-digit code. This feature can be helpful when calling branch offices and frequent customers or vendors.

Check to see if you can get a personal speed dial directory or list assigned to your telephone. This is a list of frequently called numbers that you can program and access yourself. How many speed numbers can you program? How many digits long can the speed number be? How do you program/access the speed numbers? How do you delete one? Can you store special features in a speed number, like a pause or special characters (* #)?

Many of the features available on business telephone systems today can help to make your job much easier. Taking the time to learn about your telephone can pay for itself in more effective and knowledgeable telephone use and job performance.

CHAPTER 14

Getting Organized

The Boy Scout motto says it best: "Be prepared!" The organization of your work station is key to your success as both an effective and efficient telephone professional. There are literally hundreds of books devoted to better organizational methods in the workplace. For that reason, we will stay focused on some specific ideas for the phone professional.

I will say that I have tried many different methods in my phone consultations in order to keep people focused and organized and one stands out as the most effective: Handle everything once. If you touch a file, put it in the drawer right then and there. If you have a phone message in your hand, put it in its specific slot. It sounds too simple, but in the smallest one-man operation to the largest corporation, the system doesn't have much competition. Try it.

A word has recently become trendy with auto manufacturers: ergonomics. It means having everything in its most efficient place in conjunction with everything else around you. For instance, having radio controls on the steering wheel so your hands, or eyes, always stay where they are best used. For your job, here are a few ideas for the ergonomics of your phone area.

Desk. Leaving your desk organized and clean at the end of each day is essential. Not only is it smarter, but you start each day out with minimal stress. Give yourself a large, empty place on the top of your desk that makes it easy to write at anytime.

Desk height is also important. If you have a computer keyboard, lower is better. If this is not possible, consider adding a sliding keyboard drawer or purchasing an additional computer desk.

Chair. If you spend most of the day in your chair, consider an ergonomically designed chair that is contoured to your back. A five-leg design is less likely to tilt back (or over) while you are discussing something with your boss or you are on the telephone. A chair with rollers can give you the mobility to scoot across the room to some files and return quickly if the phone rings. Overall, just be comfortable.

Telephone. The placement of your phone is just as important as what options you have available. Be sure to place your phone so that when you are using it you are able to turn away from distractions. Some executives prefer to place the telephone on a credenza so they are literally forced to turn around to handle the call.

What seems obvious to me, but is often overlooked, is that your phone placement should take into consideration whether you are right- or left-handed. It's not natural to have to reach across your desk and body to pick up the phone every time you get a call. My preference is on the right side of my desk (I'm right-handed). There it is next to my calculator. I tend to turn to my left or face a bare area when I focus on a call. Windows are not the place to look when you are trying to devote your full attention to a caller.

When choosing the phone you use, look for these convenient features:

• **Speaker phone with on-hook dialing.** This hands-free option allows you to to place a call without lifting the handset. When your party answers, you pick up. This means you can continue to work on a project while waiting for someone to answer or while holding. If you are placing a call that requires several transfers, you do not have to pick up until your party does.

If you have a speaker phone that allows two-way conversation without lifting the handset, it is proper etiquette to ask permission of the caller or person you are calling to remain on speaker.

"Mr. Brady, would you mind if we continued this conversation on my speaker phone? This will allow me to better . . . (make sure you have a justifiable reason or pick up the handset -- the sound quality is usually better anyway).

If someone is talking to you on a speaker phone and you would like them to stop, say:

"Bob, I would appreciate it if we could continue this conversation without using your speaker phone."

Politeness goes a long way.

• **Redial/Automatic redial.** Redial is readily available on most phones sold, both residential and commercial. The feature allows you to redial the last number dialed on your phone by pressing a single button. Automatic redial will continue to redial the number every 30 seconds until you get a ring.

• **Speed dial.** This feature allows you to program numbers into your phone and then only recall a 2- or 3-digit code to dial frequently used numbers. Some systems permit each station to hold private numbers while the main system is programmed to hold numbers used by many employees. If your phone doesn't have speed dial, call your local phone company. Most can now supply the extra service if you have a touch tone telephone system.

• **Conference.** This feature lets you deliver a message to several people at once. This makes sure all parties involved get the same information. What a great convenience to be able to have a telephone meeting! Once again, if your phone system doesn't provide you with this convenience, consult your local line provider.

• **Headsets.** Anyone who primarily answers phone calls should have a headset. For some reason, I find many people under the false impression that telephone operators and the folks that answer the Time/Life commercial lines are the only ones who need headsets. Telephone professionals in every line of work are now discovering how essential they are to their jobs.

Headsets offer the following additional benefits:

1. They improve your efficiency. You can get more done when both of your hands are consistently free.

2. They reduce stress by improving your posture. When you use a headset you are more likely to sit up straight because there is no need to tilt your neck and head toward the handset.

3. They allow you to fill your voice with more expression. Your hands are free to gesture, adding to the depth of your feeling and sincerity.

4. Technology has come a long way. It used to be that headsets interfered with clear conversation with static or volume problems. Now it is nearly impossible to know when someone is using a headset. In fact, in some cases, they even sound better by reducing background noise. For a list of headset providers, refer to the Resource Guide in the back of this book.

Pens/pencils. Again, it might seem like common sense that in order to take a message you would always need a writing instrument close by. I have seen plenty of desks where common sense did not prevail. Make sure you have an ample supply of sharpened pencils and/or ink pens in easy reach. I also suggest a highlighter marker for those times when you stress an important point for someone.

If your office is like most, pens have a tendency to walk off. Keep a few spares in a nearby drawer so you never have to utter, "I'll be with you in a moment. Let me find a pen!"

Paper and forms. Be sure you have plenty of the most-used forms (order forms, credit memos, etc.), message books, and paper for notes at your desk. Callers despise having to wait while you find the right form. A supply of envelopes is also handy for occasional handwritten notes. Callers are impressed and feel "special" when they receive a personalized note to confirm an appointment or a "thank you" for calling.

Mirror. Don't forget that ever so important mirror. It will show you, beyond any doubt, whether or not you are smiling and doing your job enthusiastically. If you don't like the idea of having a standard mirror at your desk -- be creative. I know a receptionist who uses the reflection of a chrome planter that sits on her desk corner.

Clock and calender. Make sure an accurate clock is easily visible from your work station (I like the fact that I have to turn around to see the clock on my credenza instead of "watching the clock" all day). A clock with an easy-to-use alarm can be helpful in reminding you of important meetings or calls.

A desk calendar or planner is helpful to have right in front of you so you can flip to your schedule, or someone else's, during any phone conversation.

Phone books/personal directory. Keep the local or most-used phone books within reach. This can be a great time saver and you will be amazed at how helpful you can be to a customer who needs a number. Remember -- always go the extra step. It sticks with people.

Consider keeping a personal directory (see Chapter 15). Mine is compiled and periodically updated on computer. In addition to phone numbers, it has addresses. We keep our "Top 100 numbers" programmed into our phone system for speed dialing. A time zone chart and a five-year calendar completes my personal directory.

CHAPTER 15

Keeping a Telephone Directory

In business it is not always what you know, but who you know and what THEY know!

During your lifetime you will meet thousands of people -- some in person and others over the telephone. Each one of them has knowledge and experiences that are potentially valuable to you and your job performance. How many times have you said, "I used to know a person who. . ."?

If you have not already, start keeping a PAL (Personal telephone and Address Listing). Your PAL, maintained properly, can be an endless source of information. You will quickly find yourself turning to your new resource many times a day to find timely answers to critical questions. While researching this book I found my PAL contained people who had instant answers to technical and statistical questions. Some I had met 10 years earlier!

Depending on your preferences, there are several types of directories; from the ever-popular Rolodex™ to a variety of manual, notebook, and computer directory systems. Most systems incorporate a "wheel" of cards. Each card contains handwritten notes pertaining to each contact. A quick spin of the alphabetically arranged wheel can solve some of the most unique or difficult questions.

Lately, I have attempted to enter the '90s by using a computer for what I used to do with a pen and a card. Again, there are several electronic devices and computer software programs that can turn your personal computer into a state-of-the-art directory. Using one of these systems with a phone modem, you can look up a contact, and additionally call the individual, with the touch of a single button. Another key stroke will allow you to keep notes on the entry.

Whatever system you choose, manual or electronic, there is some basic data you should keep on each contact*:

1. Name, correct spelling, pronunciation.
2. Mailing address.
3. Home and/or office telephone numbers.
4. Fax number.
5. Notes concerning how you met, anything that might assist you in creating or recreating an instant rapport.
6. Important dates such as birthdays and anniversaries.
7. Area of expertise.

**This information should be the minimum requirement for any entry into your directory. Depending on the entry, I keep in-depth records about the person so I can add that "personal touch" when I might need a favor.*

Harvey Mackay, nationally best-selling author of *"Swim With the Sharks Without Being Eaten Alive"* and president of Mackay Envelope Corporation, requires his sales staff to keep the Mackay 66 on each and every client. This is 66 personal- and business-related questions that allow the salesperson to easily develop rapport with any client. Your directory doesn't need to be that extensive, but knowing as much as you can will go far in helping you work more efficiently as a telephone professional.

Besides keeping the names alphabetically, consider keeping several cards on some contacts and placing them in categories. The main card should be kept where you are most likely to find it -- by last name, company name, area of expertise, or I even have some filed by first names -- as long as you can find a name and number when you need it.

Other cards should be placed in a category such as PHONE

SKILLS stating information like, "See Tony Hitt." This way, if you don't think of my name when you need information on phone skills, when you look up "Telephone Training" you will see "Tony Hitt" (I know, another plug).

Your PAL is a potential gold mine. For example, when this book was about to go to press, Kurt and I were able to do a personal mailing to colleagues promoting the book, getting sales off to a roaring start.

Give your PAL the amount of attention that should be applied to anything of such importance. Call contacts on their birthdays and holidays or send cards. Nurture your list at every opportunity, and I assure you it will come back tenfold!

CHAPTER 16

Discovering the Community Pages

Most larger Yellow Pages contain a feature that few consumers are aware of or use. It's called the Community Pages and is located in the front of your directory.

Depending on the city, the section varies in size and in the variety of information provided. The St. Louis Community Pages titled Fingertip Facts®, have emergency numbers, local attractions, maps, theatre and arena seating charts, dining and entertainment guides, calendar events, recycling information, and on and on. In addition to maps and directories, Fingertip Facts is complemented by an audio text system titled Select Talk®. This allows you to dial a local number, FREE OF CHARGE, and receive a variety of information by entering a four-digit code. In the St. Louis area, the Southwestern Bell Yellow Pages Select Talk offers information on such topics as: movie reviews, television highlights, book reviews, sports, music, nightclubs, legal, horoscopes, major city weather reports, health, stocks, financial, and real estate.

One possible business use of the Community Pages is the chance to become more familiar with cities for which business trips are being planned. Maybe you check out what is happening on your favorite soap opera while you are happily at your job (on break, of course). Check them out in your city and I am sure you will come up with many valuable uses.

CHAPTER 17

Finding Any Phone Number

Tracking down an unknown phone number doesn't have to be difficult.

Of course, for local calls you can always consult the various white and Yellow Pages printed directories. I have always found that books created specifically by the local phone companies are far ahead of those of independent companies. Accept no substitute.

For a slight charge, directory assistance is available by dialing 1-411 from any telephone that is not toll-restricted. In the case where the number you seek is in your area code, but not considered a local number, dial 1-555-1212 for assistance. If the number is in another area code, dial 1 + the area code + 555-1212. For example, for a number in the 314 area code, you would call 1-314-555-1212.

Most operators will ask you for the city in the area code you wish them to search. If they do not find the number you are requesting, ask them to expand their search to include the entire metro area or even the entire area code. If you still are not having any luck, ask the operator if there is an adjoining area code you should try. Don't worry about all the questions. It is the job of Directory Assistance to help you find the number regardless of the time it takes.

If you are looking for an "800" number, call 1-800-555-1212. I always start here when I am calling any out-of-town organization. If you are trying to find the right department at almost any major corporation, "800" Directory Assistance might have a toll-free information number for the company's own directory service. For example, you're trying to reach Citibank. They have offices all over the nation and you have no idea where to start to find the Corporate Loan Department. By calling a Citibank Directory Assistance Operator and explaining your situation, the operator will direct you to the right toll or toll-free number.

Two other lesser known resources might also be good books to have in the office: Haines® Criss Cross® and Polk Directories®. These allow you to look up phone numbers by area, address, or zip code. Both are available in most large metropolitan areas.

As with any situation, after you have found a new number be sure to record it in your PAL (see Chapter 15) for future use.

CHAPTER 18

Computers and Telephones

Technology is great! When I first started writing this book, I was well aware of the software programs available to help the big companies. There were programs to dial the phone, keep reams upon reams of records, and to keep track of the date and time someone called. I had no idea that this technology was now available for everyone -- at a price that could fit just about any budget.

If you have an IBM-compatible PC or a Macintosh with a modem, chances are you can use "Contact Management Software." The program I use, called "Sidekick™ ," allows me to keep an appointment schedule (this system has the capability to hold more than one individual's schedule -- like your boss's), a things-to-do list, and a telephone directory.

With the push of a button or two, I can review my schedule for any given day (up to the year 2099!), set alarms to go off as reminders to important appointments, keep a prioritized things-to-do list (moving all items that are not accomplished to the next day), and best of all, it keeps all of my contacts at my fingertips. My computerized PAL allows me to look up any person, and with the touch of another button, my modem dials their number. The call can even be transferred to my headset and the conversation begins. The computer can then receive notes on the call to be retrieved at any time in the future. This technology has easily doubled my efficiency (in other words, cut my previous work time in half). This is coming from a person who thought he was already well organized.

If you have access to a computer at your work station and use the phone a lot, do yourself a favor. Spend an hour or two and about $75 at your local software store. You just might leave with a program that will forever change the way you perform your job.

NOTE: "Sidekick" works in "resident memory," meaning it can be accessed regardless of whatever you are working on the computer without interfering with the current screen. This is the ultimate in computer convenience. A list of several Contact Management Software programs and companies appears in the Resource Guide section in the back of this book.

CHAPTER 19

Answering the Telephone

As you read this chapter, keep in mind that the policies and procedures recommended are targeting the widest range of businesses. It would be impossible to write a book covering every situation facing secretaries and receptionists. For instance, some very small companies prefer to answer their phones in such a way that portrays a large, established corporation. For example, "How may I direct your call" infers that there are many departments and employees in the company. On the other hand, some larger companies want to portray themselves as "mom and pop" operations -- small and service-oriented. An image of bigger or more personal can easily be conveyed by the way the phone is answered.

The way every call is handled determines whether you create business -- or lose it! Anyone who calls your company forms an impression -- positive, negative, or even indifferent -- in the first 10 seconds of the conversation. Which do you prefer? The answer is obvious, but research shows that the majority of companies are unfortunately losing potential business because they are not using their telephones correctly. Statistics tell us nearly 70% of customers who stopped doing business with a company did so because they perceived an attitude of indifference. They did not think the company gave a damn! Your attention to the following rules will determine your first impression.

There are five things which must be established in the opening seconds of a telephone conversation:

1. **Recognition and appreciation of the caller.**
2. **Company identification.**
3. **Gain and sustain control.**
4. **Convey competence.**
5. **Enthusiasm.**

This might sound like a lot to do when simply answering the phone, but let's take a look at what these items really entail.

Remember, each time before you answer put on a big smile. If you do not have this, you are already getting off on the wrong foot. Also, be prepared. When will your boss be back from lunch? What company information can you talk about? Do you have a pen available to take a message? If you are organized, you will feel good about answering the telephone anytime.

Let's take a look at the way most companies answer the phone. I would venture to guess that, if you are answering the switchboard in your company, you have used this one:

"Good morning, ABC Enterprises."

Sounds friendly enough, but there is something wrong. Chances are that if you are answering several (or several hundred) calls a day, the "good morning" part sounds about as sincere as "Have a nice day" coming from the checkout person at the supermarket.

Let's consider that you are one of those individuals who can be sincere every single time. Then, what about this situation:

"Good morning, I mean good afternoon, ABC Enterprises."

Well, which is it? You have already made a mistake in front of a potential client. No one likes doing business with people who make mistakes. Does this mean you will make a mistake when it comes to servicing his account? Probably not, but why risk it?

Still not convinced this is an incorrect greeting? Now let's assume you are always sincere and you always say "good morning" in the morning and "good afternoon" in the afternoon. If you work for a company that receives calls from all over the country, you have to deal with different time zones. It could be early afternoon for a company based on the East Coast while a customer is calling from California in the morning. It is fairly unusual to say "Good afternoon" to someone who is still drinking his first cup of coffee.

There is also another problem. I have talked to secretaries who used to say, "Good morning." They were shocked at the occasional comeback, "What's so good about it?" Yes, this is an unusual situation, but I think you will agree you don't need this extra headache during a busy day.

Here is the best alternative to taking full advantage of the first 10 seconds:

"Thank you for calling the ABC Company. How may I help you?"

or

"Thank you for calling the ABC Company. How may I direct your call?"

You have told the caller that he or she is important, reinforced your company name, and taken control of the call by asking a question. That's good for two simple sentences.

The second option, "How may I direct your call?" is recommended for switchboard operators transferring the majority of their calls and for smaller companies that wish to be perceived as large. The caller already knows that you are not personally going to handle the call. They know to just give you enough information to enable you to connect them with the correct party. This saves time and energy for both of you. If callers are upset, this could prevent them from having to retell their story of discontent more than once.

Some smaller companies prefer to have employees use their names when answering. This is fine, but consider your company's personality. Should you just use your first name or something more formal?

"Thank you for calling ABC, this is Jane. How may I help you?"

If your company name is unusually long, try dropping the "thank you for calling," but definitely leaving the question. This keeps you in control from the outset. Additionally, only abbreviate your company name if it is well-established and well-known. AT&T and IBM are excellent examples. In their particular situations, there is no need to know what these initials represent to understand what the company does.

In Chapter 26, we will talk about putting people on hold; however, let's touch on it here. If you are running a very busy switchboard and are forced to immediately put people on hold -- try answering like this:

"Thank you for calling ABC. Please hold."

or my favorite,

"Thank you for calling ABC Companies, I'll be right with you."

When you return to the caller . . .

"Thank you for holding. How may I direct your call?"

or

"Thank you for waiting. This is Bill. How may I help you?"

Recently, I called a national "800" number to place a product order and was greeted by: "Thank you for calling Acquire. Please stand by." This could also be an option. Again, you will need to make the choice based on your personality and the type of company you represent.

If your calls are usually answered at a switchboard and then transferred to you, here are a few tips. Answer your phone:

"This is Tony. How may I help you?"

or

"This is Tony."

In a department:

"Accounting. This is Kurt." or "Customer service. This is Mr.Wulff."

If the caller's name has been announced to you before the transfer, a less formal approach is appropriate. The caller has already told at least one person their name, so there is no reason to have him repeat it again while you have this information.

"Hello, Paul. This is Kurt. I'll be glad to assist you."

Allow the personality of your company and department to dictate the use of first names or more formal titles. There is a current trend which uses "Ms." in front of a woman's name, whether she is married or single. It still comes down to personal preference. Do try to avoid using only the last name when answering for yourself. "Parts Department. This is Jefferson," seems overly formal for any place other than a military installation. It's doubtful this is the image your company would like to portray.

Always avoid phrases such as, "Jim speaking." Of course you are speaking! Can you write, too? If you are answering for another person:

"Mr. Smith's office. This is Cathy."

Never answer with something like, "Joe's desk." Is Joe's desk really speaking on the phone? Of course not! We are all guilty of falling into these abrupt two-word responses, but they are incomplete and confusing. Whatever style your company chooses, make sure it is consistent and written down for anyone to reference.

While you are determining your policies, here are a few extra points that are no less important to the image of you and your company:

1. Don't allow any call to ring more than three times, even if it means immediately putting them on hold. AT&T says that callers begin to get annoyed on the fourth ring. On the other hand, answering on the first ring gives an appearance of being too eager.

2. Never use "hello" as an initial greeting. It usually confuses a caller. At a very minimum, most callers expect to hear a company name to confirm they have the right place.

3. Avoid advertisements in your greeting. For instance, this is inappropriate: "Good afternoon and thank you for calling St. Louis' original party supply company -- Clown Carnival Supply. All our costumes are half-price this week only. This is Marty. How can I help you today?"

Now why was I calling?

CHAPTER 20

Handling an Abundance of Calls

Phone professionals are placed in a variety of challenging situations -- each calling for decisive action and grace under pressure. Handling an abundance of calls is one of those situations. Here are a few tips for the times when the switchboard is overloaded with calls:

1. Stay calm. I know that is easier said than done. The point is that the more stressed you allow yourself to become, the harder it is to deal effectively with any number of calls.

2. Have a mindset to "instantly" prioritize calls.

3. Answer in the sequence the calls come into your office.

"Thank you for calling ABC Company. Can you hold?"

If "yes": *"Thank you."*

If "no": *"How may I direct your call?"*

or

"Let me have your name and number and I'll call you in five minutes."

If you don't have time to handle the occasional "no," substitute "please hold" or "please stand by" and proceed without a response. However, try the "ask first and thank you" method if at all possible. It is much more polite and the vast majority will allow you to put them on hold for a moment.

After making the rounds, return to the callers in the same sequence in which they called originally. Always thank them for holding and then regain control by asking them the appropriate question.

"Thank you for holding. How may I direct your call?"

or

"Thank you for holding. This is Diane. How can I help you?"

Sometimes when it is extra busy and you are about to pull your hair out, it becomes recognizable in your voice. You might have a tendency of being too short with a caller or flustered at the simplest request. Recently, I was sitting in my doctor's waiting room, biding my time, until he was ready to see me. I had become another victim of one of the worst flu seasons in the past five years. As I sat paging through a magazine, I listened to the receptionist answer a seemingly endless stream of calls. She answered for four doctors, setting appointments, calling in prescriptions, checking on test results -- you name it. It was just after Christmas, and they were short-staffed with people on vacation. Plus, I am guessing that the sick people who were calling were not exactly in the best of moods when she had to tell them that the doctor couldn't see them for two days. She had every reason to climb the walls to a safer place, but she did not.

To my surprise and pleasure, she never flinched. In the 15 minutes I sat and listened, the phone never left her hand, yet she handled every call with courtesy and a smile. Of course, I am sure she could not wait for lunch, but a caller would never know how badly the day was going.

Remember, when the job becomes more than you can handle, keep your attitude positive. Callers want their needs to be handled in the quickest way possible. For the most part they don't care how your day is going, nor should you tell them. Remind yourself that you are a competent telephone professional and that you thrive from the challenges you are presented with each day.

When I was on a telephone consultation some years ago, I heard the following dialogue from a secretary who was equally as swamped as my doctor's receptionist. It is another excellent model for anyone faced with an abundance of calls in a short period of time (The company name has been changed to protect the innocent).

"Thank you for calling ABC Company. Can you hold?"

"Yes."

"Thank you."

"Thank you for calling ABC Company. Can you hold?"

"Yes."

"Thank you."

"Thank you for calling ABC Company. Can you hold?"

"No."

"How may I direct your call?"

(Begins discussing a problem with an order)

"Excuse me, sir. My name is Diane. I'm the person who can assist you. However, I have two calls holding and I would not be able to give you the attention you deserve. Let me get your name and number so I can call you in five minutes."

(Gives her the information)

"Thank you, Mr. Sullivan. I'll call you in five minutes. Good-bye."

"Thank you for holding. I appreciate your patience. How may I direct your call?"

"David Cohen, please."

"One moment, I'll connect you with Mr. Cohen's office."

"Thank you for holding. I appreciate your patience. How may I direct your call?"

(She can assist him)

"My name is Diane. I can help you with that."

Of course, after that call was handled, she called Mr. Sullivan back as she had promised. Nice job!

CHAPTER 21

Holidays

Switchboard greetings can be altered during certain holiday seasons to add a little cheer. A word of warning -- be cautious when making the changes.

For New Year's, it is appropriate to say, "Happy New Year" on New Year's Day and/or the first day you are open after the holiday.

"Happy New Year from the ABC Company. How may I direct your call?"

Valentine's Day greetings are used by some retailers, but for most businesses it can probably be avoided. Even so, "Happy Valentine's Day from XYZ Gift Shop" is only appropriate on February 14. The same "exact day" policy also applies for Easter, St. Patrick's Day, Independence Day, and Thanksgiving, if your company happens to be open on these days.

The day after Thanksgiving is the best time to begin with:

"Happy Holidays from AIM. How may I direct your call?"

Depending on your business, it may be wise to avoid religious greetings. "Happy Holidays" or "Seasons Greetings" can represent the Christmas or Hannakuh seasons. Remember, never use any greeting to advertise a promotion.

Additionally, don't get ridiculous with the personal holiday touches. Mothers', Fathers', and Grandparents' Days should not be used in any greeting.

CHAPTER 22

Time Zones

As I have mentioned in a previous chapter, don't ever assume that everyone you talk to is speaking from a common time zone. Even though this might appear to be a common sense issue, embarrassing errors and miscommunication happen everyday because even the most conscientious individuals forget this point.

When talking to someone from another city, confirm that you both mean the same time. For instance, St. Louis is in Central Standard Time and our office in Cleveland is in Eastern Standard Time. Recently, I set an appointment with our trainer in Cleveland. I made sure that we confirmed whether the meeting was at 2:00 my time or 2:00 her time. This way we avoided missing each other or any other possible misinterpretations.

CHAPTER 23

Intercoming and Paging

I know what you're thinking -- another common sense chapter. Come on, everyone knows how to page someone. You might think so, but in the businesses that I have consulted, this item created some of the most embarrassing and unprofessional incidents in memory.

Paging includes the use of public address systems, intercoms, and portable pagers. Before you page anyone, ask yourself one question: Is there any remote chance that someone other than the person you are trying to reach will hear your message? If so, announce accordingly. To drive this point home, here is a story that unfortunately happened to me many years ago.

I left my office to meet a new client for a lunch meeting. I informed my staff of the location of the restaurant and that I anticipated being finished with the appointment and back on the road toward my next destination by 1:30. I could be reached by pager.

At the time I carried a voice pager. Basically, whatever my assistant said into the phone came over a speaker on my pager. Before I left the office, I had a discussion with her about a tough situation my client was going through. The client had mentioned that the family dog had died the previous evening. The lunch appointment went over about 30 minutes as we discussed our agenda. This unexpectedly put me with the client until 2:00.

At about 1:45 my voice pager sounded with the standard two beeps followed by a loud, off-key chorus of "Dead-dog Rover!" A private attempt at humor by my staff had backfired and now my client and the entire restaurant had heard it. Some thought it was funny, but the client did not.

This is an extreme situation, but the point remains: Think before you speak! Loudspeakers are not the place for jokes and ill-fated attempts at humor. You need to establish a consistent, professional style that is representative of your company's desired image. For intercom paging to someone's desk, here are a few polite tips that will keep you out of trouble.

If you know you are interrupting, or even possibly interrupting, begin with:

"Excuse me, Ms. Kelly. Would you please pick up?"

or

"Ms. Kelly, I apologize for interrupting, would you mind picking up?"

If there is no response, attempt to contact Ms. Kelly in another way, or take a message.

For in-house public address paging, use a sentence followed by a briefing. For example:

"Mr. Tyler, you have a call on line 2. Mr. Tyler, line 2."

People often don't hear the first mention. Repeating the information will help you get a quicker response. Depending on the size or purpose of your operation, you might want to use numbers to identify key people in the office. This way no one but the specific person being paged knows what is going on.

"92, please pick up on line 3. 92, line 3."

Use the same time frame as you would with the "on hold" procedures (see Chapter 26). Wait 30 seconds between a page and then return to the caller. Page again only if the caller requests it.

If on the next page there is still no response, take a message.

The number system is most popular in retail showrooms, car lots, etc., where a salesperson could be in the middle of a presentation. The call could be coming at an inopportune time. By announcing a number, the salesperson can privately decide if this is a good time to break for the call. If you had paged using his or her name, the potential client could hear this and possibly change his mind in the time the salesperson was gone. Knowing this and using numbers for employees, the salesperson can opt not to take the call.

CHAPTER 24

Screening Calls

Screening calls for another person is one of the most challenging situations in which you can be placed. On one hand, you want to be effective and do a good job for your boss. On the other hand, you don't want to jeopardize your integrity by lying to a caller.

Practiced properly, screening doesn't have to be a traumatic experience. In fact, it can and should be a positive and productive part of your position as a telephone professional. Proper screening can:

• **Help your callers get faster answers by putting them in direct contact with the appropriate person.**

• **Save you hours of interruption by eliminating the need to "brush-off" people you really don't want (or need) to talk to on certain days.**

• **Ensure that the recipient of the call is prepared to receive the call, with files and forms ready.** This allows the receiver and the caller to get more accomplished in a single call.

There are three kinds of callers:

1. People you want to talk to for any reason. This is your "Blest" list. Of course, some are more important than others. Organizing callbacks benefits you as well as the callers. Nobody wants to be involved in a phone tag situation -- not you, your boss, or those who call your company. No one has that kind of time to waste.

If your boss wants to be interrupted, transfer the caller. If a situation arises where he or she is unavailable, but left you instructions to put this person on your "Blest" list, schedule a telephone appointment.

"Hello, Mr. Brady. I'm glad you called. Mr. Hitt wants to talk with you and asked me to watch for your call. I'd like to schedule a telephone appointment so you can get connected. Is 4:00 this afternoon convenient, or would tomorrow be better?"

2. People with whom you have no desire to talk. There needs to be a clear agreement between you and your boss on with whom he will never want to talk, under any circumstance, or temporarily. This is your "Pest" list.

"Mr. Williams, I can appreciate that you believe in your product and want to talk with Mr. Hitt, but we are completely happy with our present supplier and have no interest in changing. Mr. Hitt has specifically asked me not to interrupt him with sales calls."

3. People you are not sure about given the current information (Neither on the "Blest" nor "Pest" list).

"Ms. Knox, Mr. Sedlack isn't available for phone calls right now, but I do work with him arranging callback schedules. Please tell me a little about your call and I'll do my best to help."

At this point, it might be possible to direct the caller to an individual in your organization that can better handle his call. Callers do not always know to whom they really want to talk.

On a regular basis, you and the person(s) for whom you screen should sit down and discuss updates for the "Blest" or "Pest" lists.

Once you are aware of who will be calling or who has called in the past, create a two-column format like the following example:

BLEST	PEST
Wife or husband	Unknown vendors
Some clients	Some clients
Department manager	

Besides placing the person's name on the "Pest" list, decide how to handle this caller on his next attempt. Possibilities include referring him to someone else, passing on the pertinent information to the correct individual, or discouraging future calls.

The bottom line on screening unwanted callers is the "truth." If your boss does not want to hear from him again, tell the caller. If delivered properly, and in the right tone, it will only take a few seconds -- seconds that can literally save hours. Salespeople in particular need direction. A firm "no interest now or in the future" will save the salesperson valuable time -- not to mention yourself. Simply telling the "Pest" caller, over and over again, that the person they are trying to reach is not in is just like telling them that they should call back later. What is the point?

Stop using trite responses such as "in conference" and "in a meeting." Callers rarely believe this, even if it is true, and begin forming a negative image of your company. No matter what the situation, "unavailable" is always truthful, even if the boss told you to say that he is not in the office. What if your boss suddenly hears you talking to someone with whom he does want to speak after you were told not to interrupt him? If you had said he is "unavailable," you could easily get around it by saying, "But he told me if you called, he wanted to be interrupted. One moment while I transfer you." Your credibility remains intact. Nice job!

CHAPTER 25

Transferring Calls

Depending on your position and specific responsibilities, you may or may not be able to resolve the needs of every caller. If you are a switchboard operator, chances are you may handle only a fraction of the incoming callers' needs. This chapter is designed to assist you when transferring the caller to another individual.

Most times, you will minimally need a name in order to transfer a call. Ask for the individual's name and his or her company. Sometimes you may eliminate the company and ask the reason for calling. Make these questions automatic anytime the information isn't volunteered. This will save you time and needless switching back and forth for more information. If the caller is slow to give you the needed information, try a more assertive approach:

"Sir, I will need your name before I can transfer your call."

The most basic transfer sends the caller immediately to a specific extension. The caller knows to whom he or she needs to speak .

"May I speak to James Smith, please?

"One moment, I'll connect you with Mr. Smith's office."

or

"One moment, I'll transfer you."

By repeating the name of the individual to whom you are transferring the call, the chance for misdirected calls can be greatly reduced. Also, it provides you with some mental assistance in "pushing the right button" to connect the call.

Depending on the policies within your company, it might be proper to announce your caller to the person before the transfer. This procedure, similar to screening calls (see Chapter 24), doesn't have to be complicated.

"May I (not "Can I") tell Mr. Hodge who is calling?"

"This is Mr. Eckert."

"Thank you, Mr. Eckert. I'll transfer you now to Mr. Hodge."

If the caller says "no" when you ask who is calling, respond:

"Mr. Hodge requires that I announce the caller by name before transferring any call."

or

"I will need your name to complete your call."

An abrupt "Who's calling?" gives callers the impression you are "nosy" or even worse, just plain rude. Be cautious, however, of asking a caller for his or her name only to return and tell the caller the person to whom they would like to talk is not available. True or not, the caller could believe Mr. Hodge doesn't want to talk to him or her. If you are placed in this situation, give the caller as much information as possible, for example:

"I apologize Mr. Eckert, Mr. Hodge is not available right now. I expect him to be returning calls about 3:00 today. May I take a

message?"

The other transfer situation finds the caller not certain to whom he needs to talk, for instance, on customer service calls. Some of the best customer service reps work for the Bell companies. Southwestern Bell is an excellent example of how to handle customer service calls. After identifying your situation they will place you on hold. This is when your knowledge of your organization comes into play. The Southwestern Bell receptionist contacts an individual in Customer Service. In this case we will use Mr. Wiggins.

"I have Mrs. Gerald on the line. She says she has a lot of static in her telephone. Her account number is 555-3649."

Mr. Wiggins is now aware of the situation and will not irritate Mrs. Gerald by making her repeat the problem to him. The receptionist will then return to the original caller.

"Mrs. Gerald, I have Mr. Wiggins from our service department on the line. Go ahead."

The transfer is now made and the receptionist listens until she hears both voices, thus making certain no one was disconnected. Whenever possible, let the person who will be taking the call know exactly to whom they will be speaking and the reason. As always, your responsibilities will vary depending on the policies of your employer.

If you are in the middle of a conversation with a person before you realize that you will not be able to assist him, interrupt politely using the caller's name, and let the caller know that he needs to speak to someone else. Assure him you will be happy to connect him with the appropriate person and, once again, before transferring, advise your co-worker of the situation. It might go like this:

"Mr. Eckert, excuse me for interrupting. You need to speak with our Customer Service Department. I'll be happy to connect you with someone in that department. Could you hold for a moment?"

If you are transferring to another location, as in situations when the department has its own phone number, give the caller all the pertinent information. Don't tell the caller that they might need the information if they get disconnected or transferred incorrectly. What is the caller to think -- you are someone who makes mistakes frequently? Simply explain that the information is for future use.

"Mr. Eckert, I'm going to transfer you to Customer Service. For your records, their direct number is toll-free: 1-800-555-1234."

If the person your caller asks for is not able to talk -- for whatever reason -- I suggest using the term "not available." Even if the individual is really in a "meeting," this has become a trite expression and should always be avoided. Being too specific about the requested person's whereabouts is also risky (see Chapter 33).

I am constantly amazed at what some people will tell callers -- he's in the bathroom, she's at the lake, he's STILL at lunch, she's not in the office, or he hasn't come in YET!

Repeating this information serves no positive purpose for you, your company, or the caller. As a matter of fact, if a caller is calling with a pressing matter for Mr. Hodge, and you say he is playing golf, the caller could get upset and you might lose a valuable client.

The same goes for the words "still" and "yet." Even though your boss might have been expected in at 8:00 a.m. sharp, your caller doesn't need to know that he is running a little late. Like many people, the caller might assume the worst, such as Mr. Hodge is lazy or irresponsible, never mind the fact that he might have worked on the client's project all night.

If the person is out of the office for an extended period of time, such as vacation:

"Mr. Kyle is working on an outside project (on assignment) until next Tuesday. Mr. Guest is handling his calls. Would you like me to transfer you to him?"

Yes, the project might be a "fishing trip," but the caller doesn't need to know. Your job is to make yourself and all your co-workers sound like superstars on the telephone all the time. This can only serve to improve customer relations and business. When using "not available," always follow with when they will be available. If not, you could be perceived as being curt.

One final note: Don't forget to tell Mr. Kyle what you have been saying when he returns from his trip. It could be an embarrassing situation if he returns his messages and is telling everyone that he caught a 10-lb. bass while you said he was on an outside project.

CHAPTER 26

Putting Callers on Hold

No one likes to be put on hold. Your job and the nature of business makes it a necessary, but often misused, practice. Literally thousands of current or potential customers are lost everyday because of wasted time on hold. This may have even happened to you when calling a business:

"ABC Company. May I put you hold?"

"I just . . ."

"Thank you."

Before you could even answer the receptionist's question, you are on hold -- that bottomless telecommunications pit that seems to consume the better part of our work day. The minutes seem like hours as the incessant elevator music pumps through the telephone. You think it will never end and slam down the phone totally frustrated.

This scenario might seem far-fetched, but putting a caller on hold must be handled with great care. With any call, politeness and good sense are the best things to keep in mind before putting someone on hold. Never be abrupt, no matter how busy you might be.

Recently, I have heard people substitute the words "wait" or "stand by." I still prefer "hold." It is not without some negative connotations, but it is still the most widely used. I would stay with it and play it safe. Always avoid: "Hold on!" and "Hang on!" To what? Before putting someone on hold, ask first. For instance:

"Thank you for calling the ABC Company. Can you hold please?"

If there is no answer, ask again. Never put someone on hold without waiting for a positive response. If they say "no," you have two alternatives:

1. Take care of their transfer as quickly as possible.

2. Take a message regarding where you can reach them in the next few minutes. As soon as possible, call them back and handle their request.

A caller is just looking for a commitment. Give them this, and you will head off any potential problems.

In the case that you don't have time to ask, say:

"Thank you for calling the ABC Company. Please hold."

Sometimes you have no choice. When someone is on hold, be certain that they never wait more than 30 seconds without coming back to them. Current technology now allows you to set most phone systems to ring back in 30 seconds. If your telephone is not set up to do this, keep a watch with a second hand close by. When you do return to the caller, follow this procedure:

"Thank you for holding. How may I direct your call?"

(Asks for Ms. Green)

"Thank you for holding. Ms. Green is still on the other line. Would you like to continue holding?"

If the answer is yes, put them on hold a second time. After 30 seconds, return again with an alternative and give the caller any information that might be helpful in making his next decision to hold:

"Thank you for holding. Ms. Green tells me she will be on the other line for several more minutes. May I take a message or would you like to continue holding?"

The caller will appreciate your help and honesty in this situation. If they continue holding, return in another 30 seconds, but this time don't offer an alternative:

"Ms. Green is still on the other line. Would you like to leave a message? I'll see that she gets it as soon as she is free."

Then, of course, make sure you do what you promised. In the unusual case that you are absolutely too busy to properly handle a caller on hold, still return to them within 30 seconds and say, "I'll be right with you."

CHAPTER 27

The Question of Music on Hold

There are many arguments as to what to put on hold: dead silence, music, or information. Silence makes the time on hold seem like an eternity. Music is fine, but it is difficult to please every possible caller's musical preferences. Count the number of radio stations in your city. There are as many types of music as there are different tastes. I don't think a tight-collared, senior executive calling your business would like to hear Michael Jackson while he holds. Unless you have a strictly defined target audience, you risk conveying the wrong image for your company. Also, believe it or not, your business could be at risk for licensing penalties when playing a radio station without permission over phone lines. It has happened.

My recommendation is "information on hold." The time a caller spends on the telephone is a great time to expose him to a spot commercial for your organization. Use a message like: "Thank you for holding. We appreciate your patience. The appropriate person will be right with you." Other statements can boast about company highlights, awards, etc. The messages are best with some generic, upbeat, instrumental music in the background (known as a music bed) to fill the open spaces. There are a number of excellent companies that produce these types of recordings for your phone system.

TAP Sold on Hold, located in Dallas, can provide your organization with a series of studio-produced and professionally mixed audio tapes designed to play over your HOLD button. The tapes are exclusively tailored to your company's needs, including messages regarding new products, financing opportunities, new locations, special events, and sales. The president of TAP Sold on Hold, Lawrence I. Norber, has collected extensive research on the effectiveness of "information on hold."

"Our independent researcher found that this type of service is proven to increase caller hold time by 230% while reducing hang ups by 50%. More contacts equal more sales and better customer relations."

Another twist to "information on hold" is provided by a company in St. Louis called Advertising on Hold. This concept provides callers with a full-length, 30-second commercial followed by 30 seconds of appropriate music. Dana R. Young, president of Advertising on Hold, stresses the importance of effectively utilizing the time callers are on hold.

"Research proves an average size company with six telephone lines will process 4,000 to 6,000 inbound/outbound calls per month. If half of these calls are put on hold for only 15 seconds, the total "on hold" time for the company is more than ten hours per month."

If possible, use any influence you have to make sure your company is not using "elevator music." Not only is this frequently criticized, but it is better suited for shopping malls and grocery stores.

CHAPTER 28

Taking a Message

Taking a message for someone doesn't sound overly difficult. In fact, it isn't. Most poor messages are not because we don't know what to do or how to do it, but because we are rushed or lazy. Then again, maybe it was just our attitude -- "It isn't really necessary to do it that way."

Taking messages does not have to take a long time. If you discipline yourself to always take messages in a uniform way, the time needed can be reduced. Anyway, let's say it actually does take a few seconds longer to do it correctly. How long would it take to solve a later problem if the message is in some way incomplete? For example, how long would it take to research the correct number if the wrong one is on the message?

What to Say

If you have been saying, "May I take a message?" when someone in your office is not in, you are probably missing potential business opportunities. This question makes it too easy for the caller to say no. Instead try:

"Mr. Price is unavailable. Let me have your name and number. and I will see that he gets your message."

Continue by using the "fill-in-the-blank" method:

"And your name is __________?"
"And your company is __________?"

You will be amazed how people will naturally finish the sentence for you.

Forms

Throw away those cheap pink note pads. Spend a few extra cents and get a carbonless duplicate message book (sometimes called a telephone memo book). This allows you to give the original to the person for whom the message was intended and also to retain a copy for your own records. How many times have you had someone come back to you for a number after losing his copy of the message?

I even try to review the old message books occasionally to stir up an aging contract or a forgotten name from the past. I have also been able to find "impossible" phone numbers simply by remembering the person had called me or someone in my organization months previously. Once again, make sure you retain file copies on paper or computer disk of all names and messages.

Another advantage of the book is the opportunity to track the numbers of calls and the time of day that each is received. This will give you a better idea of when to schedule breaks and possibly for scheduling additional help.

Some offices are fortunate enough to have computer-driven message systems. Messages can be input as they are received, plus a computer program offers the following advantages over traditional written messages:

1. **In most cases, you type faster than you write.**
2. **Typing is easier to read.**
3. **No paper is wasted.**

Even with this new technology, the requirements for a complete message do not change. These include:

Title: Mr./Ms. This way the message user never makes the embarrassing mistake of assuming "Chris" Thompson is definitely a woman.

First name/last name. Spell both out. If the name isn't easily pronounced, or pronounced other than it appears on paper, write it phonetically. This way you, or the message user, can always pronounce the caller's name correctly.

Company name. Write it out completely with the phone number where the caller can be reached. Avoid UK# (You Know Number). Always write a complete phone number. If the call is from any other area code than your own, include it. Plus, always ask if there is an extension that would make a return call easier.

If the caller says, "He knows the number," tell the caller that your employer insists that you always put a number on all messages. No one is interested in getting you into trouble -- they will cooperate.

Regarding. Ask what the call is regarding.

"May I tell Mr. Thompson what this is regarding so he can better prepare for the return call?"

If you make this a habit, your message users will know that when there is nothing in the "Regarding" section, that the caller did not wish to leave the information. This will assist in appropriately handling any potential call backs.

Avoid short phrases like "What's this about?" or "What's this regarding?" These expressions can make you appear more nosy than efficient. Be polite.

If the caller says it is "personal," write this on the message. If I get a message that says "personal" or "old friend" on it, and it turns out to be a devious salesperson, the relationship is immediately terminated. Once again, my assistant has saved me valuable time.

Check the boxes. Those boxes on the side of the form, such as "Returned your call," are there for a reason. Use them! There is no need to write out in long hand what can be said with a check mark (✓).

Date/time: This allows the message user to act accordingly. If I get a message from Mr. Jones that was taken at 10:30, and I talked to him at 11:15, there is no need for me to return the call. If the message taker had only written a date, I would have embarrassed myself, the company, and the message taker by calling again.

Initials. Finally, your name or initials should appear somewhere on the message. This might not be as important in smaller businesses, but it is still a good habit. If the message user has a question, he or she immediately knows who to talk to about the incoming call. Everyone appreciates saving time.

Closing

After you have taken all the pertinent information, let the caller know that you will make sure that the correct person gets the message. A sample close would be:

"I'll see that Mr. Taylor gets the message."

Never say:

"I'll make sure Mr. Taylor returns your call."

Unless you plan to stand over Mr. Taylor with a gun, you should never make a promise that you cannot control. If you need to be more assuring, try:

"I'll personally make certain Mr. Taylor gets the message the minute he returns."

This is something you can do. Only make promises you can keep. Never make a promise someone else has to keep and, of course, keep the promises you make.

By using the book, and the described procedures religiously, you'll quickly become known as someone whom employees trust. Your co-workers will never have a reason to blame you for forgetting a call or message. No message in the book – no call.

Where Do They Go?

Again, it sounds simple, but message memos should have one, established location. I like a "message wheel." It can be purchased for about $20 at most office supply stores. It allows you to keep messages for about 25 people in a 9-square-inch space on your desk. It also enables message users to pick them up at the same place.

"Take it and place it" -- handle it once. If a message user has not picked up his or her messages in awhile, it is easy for you to tell repeat callers that the message user has not received the message yet.

In the situation when the message user calls from the field and you read the message to him or her, place an "X" over it to let you know that the message has been given. Then replace it in the wheel for the message user to later pick up.

Never use scratch paper for messages! This increases the chances for lost and incomplete messages. Always have your "message book" handy. If necessary, have more than one book. Doing it the same way and on the same form ensures accuracy and saves time.

CHAPTER 29

Wrong Numbers

The following information might seem obvious to you. If so, great! You're ahead of the majority of the country.

When you answer a call and the caller has reached you by mistake (misdialed, been given the wrong number by an associate, etc.) treat them with respect and with the same courtesy you would give to any other caller. Here is why:

1. You have just told the caller the company name. Would you prefer to:

A. Tell them off or hang up without any comment. This would give them the impression that your organization treats "everyone" this way.

B. Assist the caller as much as possible, letting them know that your company always goes the extra step for callers/customers. There could be that outside chance that this caller might need your product or service in the future and will remember your assistance.

2. Doesn't it make you feel good to voluntarily help someone? Sure it does.

If you often get calls for a company that has changed its number or gone out of business, tell the caller any information you have collected.

"No sir, this is ABC Plumbing. XYZ Printing moved about a year ago. I believe their new number is 555-2345.

Likewise, when you reach a wrong number be polite and apologize for the interruption.

"I believe I misdialed. I apologize for the interruption. Thank you."

Can this really increase your business? The answer is yes. My accountant is proof of this. She receives many calls for a large local department store because of a similarity in telephone numbers. In a casual, friendly way, she lets the callers know that she is an income tax preparer and encourages the caller to remember "the wrong number" at tax time. Of course, after this soft sell, she gives them the number for the department store. Her techniques have resulted in new clients, and naturally, increased income.

CHAPTER 30

In Person vs. On the Telephone

This brief chapter deals primarily with those individuals, such as retailers, who work with the public. Even though I believe all telephone calls should be handled with the utmost attention, I have an opinion about customers in a store.

A customer in a store always takes priority over a caller on the phone (a bird in the hand is worth more than two in the bush). If you are in a position where you wait on customers at a counter and also are answering incoming calls -- take my advice. Give priority to the person who is present in the store. There is nothing more annoying than standing at a checkout counter ready to pay for purchases, and the salesclerk is busy answering questions on the telephone. When you are placed in this tough situation, excuse yourself from the customer for one moment, answer the phone before the third ring, and let the caller know:

"I am with a customer right now. Would you like to hold for ___________ (give an honest assessment of the time needed) or can I take your number and call you back in (same amount of time)?"

When you return to the in-store customer, thank them for waiting. Of course, return the call as promised when you are finished with the customer.

Another point worth noting (this one drives me crazy when I

witness it): When you finish a call do not make degrading remarks about the caller or appear to be frustrated by the interruption. The person standing at the counter might be your phone customer next week, and you would not want them to think you talk about every call that way.

CHAPTER 31

Saying "Good-bye"

When all of your business is complete, and it's time to end the call, there are still a few things to consider.

As we covered earlier, the first several seconds of a call set the stage and sometimes even an entire relationship. The last seconds are no less important. You don't want to destroy everything you have established in your conversation with the wrong choice of words. What if you sound angry or insincere because you hung up too loudly?

Most residential callers believe that the individual who originated the call is the one responsible for ending the call. This might be true if you are at home, but business is different. In most cases, I believe the receiver should maintain the upper hand on this decision. In either case, always thank the other person.

"Thank you for calling today, Mr. Jones. I'll be sure to send the information out in today's mail."

or

"I appreciate your bringing this to my attention, Mr. Williams. We'll make sure it doesn't happen again. Thank you for calling."

If you desire an indication from the other party that the call is indeed over, wait for it. If on the other hand, you are trying to wrap the call up quickly, go on to a close. What is a close? Just say "good-bye."

A simple "good-bye" before you hang up is simple and pleasant. Some telephone professionals believe that it is not necessary and that you should just hang up after the "thank you." Even though it might not be necessary, it has come to be expected in today's business environment. Without it, you sound rude or abrupt.

On the other hand, don't take it too far. "Bye-bye" does not belong at the end of any business conversation. It immediately lowers the other person's perception of you as well as your company. Men sound especially odd when uttering "bye-bye."

Slang or shortened expressions such as "later," "see ya," or "bye" should also be avoided. At the very least, they are unprofessional and you risk sounding cavalier.

For those who would like to put themselves above the average customer service professional, add the following question right before you thank the caller:

"Is there anything else I can help you with today?"

This shows the caller that you are genuinely concerned about getting to the heart of his or her needs. Even if the caller was originally calling to voice dissatisfaction, this offers one more reassurance that you are dedicated to going the extra step to please him or her. If they come back with another complaint, it is another opportunity for you to serve a valuable client and continue to get their business for your company.

One last point before the call ends: Let the other party hang up before you do. Make sure you hear it. Have you ever had "just one more question" for someone, and you did not think of it until the moment you were hanging up? Most of us have. Therefore, by waiting until the other party hangs up first, you ensure that they are not left hanging with unanswered questions. And when you do hang up, do it gently.

CHAPTER 32

Handling Complaints

No one wants to have an upset customer, but handled correctly, they can be transformed into your best customers. I've seen it happen.

Actually, I like handling complaints. Hold on, I do not mean that my company has a lot of problems, but I see an occasional complaint as a challenge instead of an uncontrollable situation. The best analogy I know is looking at the initial complaint as the kickoff in a football game. Like football, there are strategies and rules to be followed. There is even a chance to score extra points. Fortunately, in our version, no one has to lose. Your goal is to satisfy the customer or client with a resolution that is mutually agreeable. When you succeed in this goal, the customer should generously be willing to recommend your company's services to others.

Prepare. This means placing yourself in an alert posture and focusing on the caller -- turning away from all distractions. How many times have you listened to a caller's "story" and your mind began to wander? The one small detail you missed could be pertinent to solving the problem.

Have all your forms ready and be prepared to record all the information dictated to you by the caller. Stay away from any mention of "filling out forms or writing down all of the information for the record." This could sound like another hurdle for a caller who is looking for a quick solution to a complaint.

NOTE: If you use a computer, being prepared includes having your computer in the correct program and on the correct screen.

Listen and empathize. In an earlier chapter, we talked about listening for the real meaning behind the words. Place yourself in an adult frame of mind -- one that is unbiased to the points that will be raised about you or your company. As you listen, put yourself on the other end of the telephone. What if you were in the caller's position? Offer feedback and encouragement by using phrases like, "I understand . . ." or "I can appreciate that . . ."

Be sure to take good notes. At no time should the caller have to repeat something. Each time the problem is restated, there is a snowball effect, and the problem grows out of proportion. Have you ever called a company with a seemingly simple concern, only to have your call misdirected countless times? You became angrier each time you were forced to repeat your entire story. The fact that someone has to repeat what has already been explained sends out a signal that the complaint is not important. If you need to transfer the call, be sure to pass on the caller's story to the correct individual so the problem can be handled quickly and efficiently.

A couple of years ago, in the dead of winter, I received a "Disconnect" notice from the local electric company. Knowing I had already paid the bill, I called their main service number. When I called, the phone rang three or four times, then a recording came on telling me to hold -- a representative would be right with me. I waited for what seemed to be an eternity. Finally, a real person answered. I told the rep about the notice and that it had been paid. She let me continue to tell her that I was going out of town and that I wanted to make sure I had service when I returned. I went on to explain that I had an aquarium and plants. If I lost my power, I would lose my fish and freeze my plants.

At this point, she asked me my address. She then followed with, "Oh, you have to call another office." Fifteen minutes had now elapsed and I was becoming angry. When I called the other number, I got the same number of rings. The same recording. The same wait.

Someone finally answered. I immediately told her my address, but wasn't as friendly this time. She, in turn, also sounded irritated. I told my story again. I told her about the notice, my payment and about my flight which was leaving in an hour and a half. Yes, I even told her about the sad fate that awaited my fish and my plants.

She proceeded to place me on hold to check my records! After several more minutes, she returned. She explained that the payment had not been credited to my account. Worse yet, before she asked any questions, I was ordered to get the payment in by 10:00 the next morning, in person, or my power would be cut. Guess where I was supposed to go to make the payment -- the office I had called first!

Now I was fuming! My fish! My plants! What are my alternatives? The rep was real helpful here. She explained that I had no alternatives. I had to make the payment or I could kiss my fish and plants good-bye. I asked for the supervisor.

Surprise! I had to wait again for several more minutes. When the supervisor came on, I was forced to tell my story one more time, but now I was yelling.

"Listen, buddy, I'm late for my flight. I have absolutely no time to make a duplicate payment because someone at your stupid company misposted my check."

For added emphasis, I told this guy that my kids were sick with the flu, my wife was about to divorce me, and if they turned off my electricity, my life would end! After these desperate pleas, finally someone made an honest effort to help me. The supervisor informed me that he would make a note on my account if I would mail another check that day. I agreed.

After spending nearly half an hour on the phone, now I was angry that the solution was so simple. Why hadn't someone done this first? Why did I have to tell my story so many times? I mailed my check and my non-existent wife and kids survived.

The fact that someone has to repeat what has already been explained sends out a signal that the complaint and the caller are not important. If you need to transfer the call, be sure to pass on the caller's story to the correct individual so the problem can be handled quickly and efficiently.

Create rapport. Once again, one of the best ways to start is by empathizing with the caller's position. Earlier we talked about rapport, and in complaint situations superior rapport skills are essential. You need to find common ground. Remember, your goal needs to be the same. You both want the caller to be satisfied with the resolution. From the outset of your conversation, start off on the right foot:

"Mr. Hill, we have at least one thing in common. We both want to find a satisfying solution to your situation."

Continue to use the caller's name as often as possible. This is a personal touch that will go a long way in calming a storm. Your aim should be to become the caller's partner, sharing his or her concerns. Only by solving the complaint will this be accomplished. Before the call ends, clarify the real problem by making sure you use six words that are the favorites of journalists: who, what, when, where, why, and how (see Chapter 12). These questions mean that you genuinely care to learn more about the caller's situation.

Negotiate or create a solution. Remember what your objective is: To come to a mutually agreeable solution. Do not get into a tug of war with the client over who did what and who is at fault. The simple fact is that something has happened that needs your attention. Arguing will never solve the complaint because you cannot win. If you lose the argument, the caller's complaint was accurate and you look foolish trying to argue your case. If you win the argument, the caller is proven wrong and will probably be angry enough to never do business with you again. Avoid the finger pointing and get to the root of the problem as quickly as possible so you can create a solution. How do you do this?

Come right out and ask what the caller wants you to do. If you can do it, then handle it. The problem is solved. If the situation is more complicated, explore the options. Research shows that every satisfied customer tells approximately 3 people about your company. On the other hand, every dissatisfied customer tells a minimum of 11 others about his dissatisfaction. Think about the awesome potential each call holds for your business. Don't take chances.

Confirm your information. Be sure you and the caller are on the same wavelength. Make a point of verifying all addresses, phone numbers, and spellings. Review with the caller the action steps that need to be taken by each party. In some situations it might be necessary to include putting them in writing.

Follow through. Keep every promise you make and do not make a promise you cannot keep. The credibility of every company hinges on fulfilled commitments. If you say you will call a client in 10 minutes with an answer -- do it! If you still don't have the information you need to give them, call them in 10 minutes anyway and provide them with an update as to when you will have the information. This type of follow-through communication is appreciated and rarely forgotten. The last thing you want is an irate caller to be forced to call you back. Developing rapport is nearly impossible at this point.

By using this system, you will quickly gain the confidence to turn any disgruntled caller into a satisfied customer.

Extra points. This is your chance to go even further beyond effective follow-through. It means instilling a special feeling in the previously disgruntled customer that makes him confident to do business with you again -- and even recommend your products or services to others.

A couple of years ago, I purchased a car from a Lou Fusz auto dealership in St. Louis. Lou Fusz represents one of the largest auto networks in the Midwest.

After driving it for a few months, the cold start switch blew out (the engine would not immediately turn over when the key was turned). I immediately called the Service Department at Lou Fusz and set up an appointment for the next morning. At that time, I was met by a service representative who explained that the repair was under warranty and that there would be no charge. He explained that he understood my inconvenience with such an unexpected repair in a new car and assured me that it would be ready at the lunch hour.

At 11:00 that morning he called to tell me that the car was ready as promised. I went over during my lunch hour and was greeted by the same representative who made sure the car was pulled around to the front of the building where I waited. He provided me with a thorough explanation of the repairs and told me to call if I needed anything else.

Even at the times I wanted to be angry -- I couldn't. The rep had handled all of my concerns even before I had made them apparent. On top of this, I received a call exactly 30 days following the repair work from the same Service Department. I was greeted by a friendly voice that explained he was following up on the work and wanted to make sure I was still satisfied. With a simple phone call, they earned the extra points to create a loyal customer. I highly recommend their services to friends and family at every opportunity.

CHAPTER 33

Handling Aggressive or Inquisitive Callers

Who qualifies as an aggressive caller?

This is a person who asks for an unusual amount of information about your company -- more information than you are authorized to give. Some of the familiar questions include:

- **Where is your boss?**
- **How much business did you do last year?**
- **How many salespeople do you have?**
- **What do you do?**

Often they are the friendliest people you will talk to, but at the same time, they throw a seemingly endless line of questions at you. What are you supposed to say in these situations? First of all, know exactly what you can and cannot say over the telephone. The fact is, each company's policy will vary concerning the handling of such questions. Make a point of sitting down with your office manager or top management to find out what your specific policies are. Learn what is public information and what is not. Write a clear, concise statement that explains what your company does. Make a list of the most commonly asked informational questions. Write down the answers you are allowed to give. Any information not included in your written answers is considered out-of-bounds. Next to each question note the name of the individual in your company who can be contacted if the caller crosses the line. The next time a caller asks you one of the questions, politely recite your prepared answer, word-for-word, off your sheet. The moment the caller becomes aggressive, refer them to the contact for that question:

"I'm not privileged to that information. I can transfer you to Ms. Williams in that department. Would you like to hold?"

or

"I can transfer you to the president of the company. Can you hold?"

Nine times out of ten you will hear a dial tone before you hear another word. This is because the caller asking these questions is usually a salesperson on a fact-finding mission before contacting a certain person in your company. There are a few exceptions to the rule. The majority of companies will allow you to mention any type of public or published information. This includes the names of officers in the company and your specific address. Anything that is public record should be handled quickly and without further screening. Do not waste your time trying to find out why they want to know. This information includes items such as the president's name and the mailing address. Just give it to them, but know when to stop. Just because you have insights into the company and its personnel doesn't mean everyone needs to know.

Giving out too much information can be dangerous. For instance, what if the employee asked for is out of the office? The caller then continues:

"When do you expect him back?"

"Not until next week. He's on vacation."

The caller doesn't need to know where the employee is at that given moment. From personal experience, I have heard receptionists dig themselves even deeper because they did not know when to stop.

"Yes, he's on vacation for the next 10 days. The lucky guy went to Hawaii with this wife and kids. He deserved the break."

The literal translation of this information could be, "His house is empty over the next week. Feel free to stop by and clean him out." Sound ridiculous? There have been several documented cases where thieves used the phone and unwitting receptionists to set up their hits. Realistically, if the caller has a problem, does he or she really need to hear that the person who can solve that problem is on a beach? The best reply is still:

"Mr. Simmons is not available."

or

"Mr. Simmons is unavailable right now. I do expect him to return calls around 2:00. . ."

or

"Mr. Simmons is working on an outside project until next week, however, Mr. Reynolds is taking his calls. May I transfer you or would you prefer to leave a message? I expect Mr. Simmons to return calls on Monday."

The key in dealing with aggressive callers is to know what <u>not</u> to say, as well as what <u>you will say</u>. Find out today what your company policies dictate when someone is out of the office.

CHAPTER 34

Handling Long-Winded Callers

Did you ever have a caller that seemed to be telling you his life story? Some people use every opportunity to talk as much as possible. These are the callers who either cannot get to the point when you answer the telephone or do not allow you to hang up when your business is complete. How can you wrap it up without being rude? Being courteous and patient is certainly important, but not in excess. Your time is valuable and needs to be equally distributed to each caller.

There is one line that is extremely effective in getting a caller to come to the point. At the first opportunity, say:

"What can I help you with today, Mr. Roberts?"

or

"How can I assist you, Mr. Roberts?"

Avoid any other open-ended questions or pauses of silence. The caller will probably fill these blanks in for you and all of a sudden you have lost control.

Of course, there is the instance when you have finished helping the caller as much as possible, yet he wants to continue the conversation. This can be particularly damaging and irritating when your other lines are ringing. To end the call, begin talking in the past tense.

"I've enjoyed our conversation, Mr. Roberts, and I'm glad you called. I'll send the information out in today's mail."

If this is still ineffective, continue with:

"Mr. Roberts, I must take another call now. Is there anything else I can do for you today?"

In extreme situations, take complete control.

"Mr. Roberts, I've really enjoyed our conversation today, I'll be sure to mark your account as we discussed. Thank you for calling."

Then disconnect. Even though it is sudden, the caller will understand if it is handled smoothly.

CHAPTER 35

Handling Abusive or Threating Callers

There is no room in any business setting (or personal for that matter) for profane or threatening remarks. This goes for you or the caller. Find out what your company's policy is on abusive situations. Once again, if you do not have a written policy, consider these practices.

This is an excellent example of where the customer is not always right. At the moment the caller becomes rude or vulgar, firmly take control by using the caller's name. If you know the last name, use it instead of the first. This puts you in a better business posture and denotes your seriousness. The following is a three-step process for dealing with the most aggressive callers:

Step 1: *"Excuse me, Mr. Andrews, your language is making it very difficult to concentrate on your situation." (At no time should you raise your voice)*

Step 2: *"Mr. Andrews, if you continue with that type of language, I will have no alternative but to disconnect the line."*

Remember, callers want reliable and dependable service. That means phone operators who keep their promises. Disconnect the abusive caller if he or she continues in the same manner after your warning.

Step 3: If they call back, treat them like a new caller until they start again (hopefully they won't start again). If they do, skip back to Step 1 and repeat the process.

In most cases, you will not have to go beyond the first two in order to calm the situation. On those rare occasions when the bad language or threats continue after step 2, do not be afraid to proceed with a disconnect. At no time should it be in your job description to tolerate such rude behavior. There is no place for it in business and no excuse for it.

As a back up, make sure you report the incident to your supervisor immediately. I recommend a simple "incident form" or more appropriately, a CYA (Cover Your Assets) form. This allows you to write down the report, word for word, if possible. Detail what the caller said, what you said, and the disconnect if used. Give a copy to your boss and put one in your files. If the caller calls back to report you, you have beaten him or her to the punch.

CHAPTER 36

Handling Hard-to-Understand Callers

Many large companies take calls everyday from all parts of the country -- even internationally. Sometimes this causes difficulties in communication, including differing dialects or strong accents that create "broken English." When I raised this point in a recent seminar, two participants informed me that these were not the only individuals who are hard to understand.

"Did you ever talk to an engineer when he is using the jargon of his profession?" the first lady asked.

Before I could answer, the next lady continued, "Our company does a lot of contracting with architects. I had one call the other day and I had to ask him to repeat himself at least four times before I could decipher his technical lingo."

Obviously, industry jargon can be just as confusing, and the same rules apply when trying to handle these hard-to-understand callers.

Sometimes it is not the language that confuses us. Sometimes it is just the rate of speech. Those from the deep South often talk slower than we are accustomed to in the Midwest. On the other hand, someone from the Northeast might pose an equally taxing challenge by speaking very quickly and bluntly. Add to this that both regions will also use unique geographical sayings, and you have a lot of room for potential confusion and mistakes on the telephone.

If you are faced with someone who, for instance, talks faster than you, use the concepts we talked about early in this book. Try reverse mirroring to build rapport. In this situation, start speaking slower. Often this will be an effective indication for the other person to slow down. Mirroring then becomes a dual participation.

If after much work, you still find it nearly impossible to comprehend what is being said, politely interrupt and ask the caller to repeat himself. Ask him to spell words or even phrases that you do not understand. Chances are, if you are having problems understanding the caller, this has happened to him before and he will try to help you as much as possible.

CHAPTER 37

Placing Calls

Placing Calls for Yourself

There are three main parts to placing a phone call. You will recognize each point as part of previous subjects covered in this book, but they bear repeating.

First, you need to have an objective. When the call is completed, what do you want to have gained from the communication?

Second, focus all your attention on the phone call at hand. Do not allow events happening around your work area to distract you.

Third, and most importantly, have an agenda. Know exactly what you want to discuss and how you want to go about it. Your goal should be never to hang up the phone and say, "Oh! I wish I had asked her about . . ." Try making a list of the individuals whom you call the most in a month's time. Each time you think of an item you need to discuss with a certain individual, write it down underneath his name, maybe on a card. When you make contact, even if the individual called you, pull the card and go point-by-point down the card until your agenda is complete. Once it is you can confidently end the call knowing you made the best use of your time and that of the other individual.

Placing Calls for Another Person

When placing a call for another person (your boss, another employee, etc.) a certain degree of etiquette and common courtesy should be maintained. Before you place the call, make sure that the person for whom you are placing the call is ready. Then go ahead.

"Ms. Charles, do you have a minute to speak with Mr. Hitt?"

"Yes."

"I'll connect you now."

Depending on the purpose of the call, it may be appropriate to tell the contacted party the objective of the call so files or notes can be readied.

Having someone place your calls for you can be a great time saver. However, if you have someone place a call for you, respect the individual you are calling and be on the line within 10 seconds. It is not only rude, but pretentious, to presume your time is more valuable than that of the person you are calling. Considering this fact in reverse, if you happen to be holding for someone not placing his own call, disconnect anytime someone makes you wait an inordinate amount of time.

CHAPTER 38

Placing International Calls

Because of the significant extra cost of international calls, it is more important than ever to be prepared. With that in mind, let's examine the technical aspects of such calls.

Just a few years ago, you would have to dial for operator assistance for any international phone call. However, following so many other trends in society for self-service, now overseas calls are just a matter of dialing a few more numbers.

First, you will need to know your country's access code. This will give you the overseas network you will need to complete the call. In the United States, the AT&T code is 011.

The next series of numbers is the country code. This will be 1 to 3 digits and can be acquired from your local phone company.

Now you are ready to dial the correct city and actual individual you are trying to reach. The city code will be the next set of numbers and can be compared to the area code system used in the United States.

Then, of course, the last set of numbers is the actual phone number. Depending on the country, the number of digits will vary so don't be worried that you have the wrong number or have too many or too few digits.

These calls can be confusing, so if you ever need any assistance, an international operator will be glad to lend an understanding ear.

CHAPTER 39

About Pagers

Even though pagers have been mentioned at other places in this book, there are a few technical points to be made. There are several types of pagers and several uses.

1. Tone pagers. This type of pager emits a "beep" or vibrates when the number is dialed. This signals the person with the pager to call a pre-designated number for messages.

2. Voice pagers. This type of pager "beeps," but then is followed by the caller's voice. This one-way transmission allows the caller to tell the person holding the pager an exact message and whether or not a return call is necessary. You have the message immediately and there is no need to call the office.

3. Digital pagers. This pager signals the holder with a "beep." This pager allows the caller to push in the number the paged individual needs to call. The number then appears on the pager for quick access. To further enhance the use of this type of pager, try using priority codes along with the number. Instruct the person who will be calling your pager to add a single number code after each transmitted phone number. Most digital pagers have a display that allows you to enter 10 numbers (an area code and a phone number.) If most of your calls are local, you will not need to enter an area code. Use this available space for your code. You might use:

1 = Call Now!
2 = Call as soon as possible.
3 = Not a priority. Call when available.

4. Data pager. This is the newest innovation in the pager line. It allows a service, or a caller with the proper equipment, to leave a complete message on a digitally controlled screen. This is the most comprehensive of the pager types. It allows you to receive everything that might be included in a printed phone message: names, addresses, phone numbers, and exact messages.

Because this type of pager is usually billed by the digit, it might be a good idea to abbreviate and code messages to some extent.

CHAPTER 40

About Cellular Telephones

When cellular telephones were first introduced, it seemed that the highest paid executives and dignitaries were the only individuals who were allowed access -- they were just too expensive for anyone outside this elite circle. Today, cellular technology makes it affordable for almost anyone to have a portable telephone. Besides the obvious uses and time-saving possibilities for business people, cellular telephones are now commonly used by students, housewives, and retirees.

The investment for the telephone itself has become minimal. As a matter of fact, the gas station I frequent will give away a portable car telephone after 10 fill-ups. A representative of Southwestern Bell Mobile Systems in St. Louis tells me that a cellular telephone can be activated and ready for usage for about $20 per month. Of course, you still pay a premium price for each minute of usage. Additionally, many people like the security of having the telephone for emergency use. With a car phone, if you break down or have an accident, you do not even have to leave your car to call for assistance.

Whatever your use for a mobile phone, keep in mind that you pay for both your incoming and outgoing calls. Give out the number sparingly and make it clear which calls are important enough to warrant the expense.

After looking at the amount of a cellular usage bill, a pager might be warranted also. A pager will allow you to know who is trying to contact you. Plus, if they are using a priority code (see Chapter 39), you can make the decision if the call needs to be returned via your mobile phone or if it can wait until you return to your office. Besides being a nice way to screen potential cellular calls, the pager serves as a nice back-up if your portable phone is battery-powered and running low on energy. This way you won't miss that important call.

I have heard it said recently that telling the person you are calling that you are speaking on a car phone is viewed as pretentious. "Not so," says Stuart Crump, publisher of the *Cellular Sales and Marketing Newsletter* and a columnist for *The Mobile Office Magazine.*

"Let it slip that you are calling from your car, not to impress them, but to let them know this is a business call. Cellular calls still give the impression that long distance phone calls used to convey: This is an important call. You will find you are on the phone a much shorter time."

CHAPTER 41

About Fax Machines

In recent years, there have been many exciting innovations in business equipment technology. One of the most revolutionary inventions is the facsimile machine, better known as the fax. As more and more companies enter production on these machines, the prices are dropping quickly. A fax machine is now becoming as essential to a company as the telephone and copy machine, and depending on the model and options you choose, it can be very affordable. Home usage is also rapidly increasing.

I seem to come up with a new use for the fax machine everyday. People are becoming so accustomed to fax machines that letters are written and faxed instead of mailed. Instantly an important letter can be in the hands of your client. Imagine the postage and overnight costs you save. Short faxed notes are replacing calls. This can be a great way to eliminate telephone tag. Try writing a note in a "fill in the blank" form, fax it, and wait for the response.

Even though the fax is now a widely accepted practice, the system is not without an occasional bug. It is not a bad idea to call to confirm that the party you were faxing has received it or is even aware it was sent. Often fax machines are shared by several departments within a company and are quite a distance from your target. Many companies are still trying to organize the way that fax transmittals are collected and delivered. This might mean your fax could sit in a tray for a day or two without going to the appropriate person. This does not seem like the best method if you need a quick answer.

I would strongly recommend always using a fax cover sheet. To save paper you can use a half sheet that has a space for the following information:

- **Company name of sender**
- **Company name of receiver**
- **Individual receiving**
- **Fax # of receiver**
- **# of pages including cover**
- **Individual sending**
- **Fax # of sender**
- **Telephone # of sender**
- **(A space for notes or additional comments)**

Always be aware of how much paper you are sending and try not to be wasteful. Some advertisers have recently discovered the fax machine as a new medium for their product. If you are receiving junk facsimiles that you don't want, call the sender and tell them you are not interested. It is your paper they are using and you have a right to protest.

This relatively new technology has raised various legislative questions and debates in states across the country. A New York civil court judge recently ruled that fax machines can be used to serve papers, such as court orders, to a litigant or his lawyer during the course of a case.

Similar legislation and regulations are being hotly contested regarding the use of facsimiles for unrequested and unwanted advertising promotions.

CHAPTER 42

About Automated Attendants

"Can you explain how auto attendants work?"

"To find out how they work, please press one."

Okay, I press one.

"To find out how to use auto attendants, press one. To find out why so many people dislike this system, press two . . ."

What is an automated attendant? Maybe an example would best explain.

Your boss has told you to call a company in town, for instance one of the utilities, and gather some billing information. You dial and a recorded message answers:

"Thank you for calling Big Electric. If you know the extension you are calling and are at a touch tone phone, you may punch in the number anytime during this message. If you need customer service, push 1. If you are . . ."

And on and on and on. As irritating as this technology might be, for some companies it is the best system. There are several benefits including:

• **Calls can be answered and processed more quickly -- most are set to answer on the first ring.**

• **Calls can be processed 24 hours a day, seven days a week, even at times when a live attendant would not be available, or when the**

switchboard would not likely be open. This allows employees who do not have published numbers to receive direct calls at any time. Automated attendants can significantly reduce the call volume that is handled by the live attendant, therefore allowing more time to take care of those callers who really need operator assistance.

• **The system can also be used to back-up live operators at peak periods, or when they take a break.**

However, there are some negatives to be considered:

• **Only those callers with touch tone phones can take advantage of the call-directing features.** Others must wait and be handled as a "default," when their calls are usually routed to an operator. After working hours, default calls are usually just routed to a general mailbox, where they can only be processed the next day.

• **Some callers may miss the personal touch of having their calls answered by a live person.** Many companies experience about a 1% complaint rate when implementing an automated attendant. Most of the complaints are simply from those who do not like being answered by a "machine."

Getting Started

If your company is planning to install an automated attendant, use these simple guidelines to make life easier for your callers:

1. **Make sure the system is programmed so that a caller who requests a live attendant by dialing "0" can reach one during normal working hours, and make sure that the greeting (the recorded message) specifies that "0" can be dialed at any time during the announcement.** Do not allow the system to send callers into an endless loop or repeated menu when they need personal assistance.

2. Be certain that, during normal working hours, those callers who don't have touch tone phones can reach a live attendant. Additionally, make sure that the greeting instructs them to "stay on the line for operator assistance."

3. Keep menus short so calls can be processed quickly and in order that callers are not overwhelmed with choices.

4. Do not have too many levels or menus.

5. Put the most frequently called departments or choices at the top of the menu.

6. Program the system to give callers an option to reach a company directory. This will ask them to key in the name of the person they are trying to reach.

The following is a sample of a typical company main menu:

"Thank you for calling XYZ Company. If you know the extension of the party you are trying to reach, you may dial it at any time during this announcement. To reach an operator, dial "0" at any time. For Field Service, dial 1. For Marketing, dial 2. For Accounting, dial 3. For a company directory, dial 9. Or, stay on the line for operator assistance."

How to Use It

Now, how do you deal with an automated attendant when you are calling a company? First of all, be patient, but here are a few more tips:

• **You can almost always dial "0" to reach a live attendant.** If you do not know your party's extension, or you know you need assistance, hit "0" as soon as your call is answered.

• **Use the company directory feature or dial-by-name feature, if available.** This can be particularly helpful in getting around secretarial screening, especially outside normal business hours.

• **If you are not calling from a touch tone phone, just wait on the line patiently.** At the end of the greeting, your call will be routed automatically. If you cannot get touch tone service, you can buy small, inexpensive (about $15), hand-held DTMF pads for use with automated attendants, voice mail, and answering machines.

CHAPTER 43

About Voice Mail and Answering Machines

Although many of us despise the various answering services used today, they do serve an important purpose if used correctly. We will look at both sides of this technology, but first, a few tips before you record your message.

1. Keep it current. Let callers know how long you may be away from your telephone and be specific, rather than leaving a generic message, if possible. Some companies even require their employees to update their greetings daily.

2. Most voice mail systems allow the caller to dial "0" (or on some systems 0#) to get out of a voice mailbox, if they need to speak with a person. However, many of the systems do not prompt the caller that they have this option. Your recorded greeting should let the caller know that he should dial "0" to return to an attendant for personal assistance. The key is always to make it as convenient as possible for the caller to be helped.

3. Use your outgoing message to encourage your callers to leave complete messages so that you are better able to help them when you return their calls.

4. Check to see where your calls are routed if a caller does dial "0" while in your mailbox. Most systems allow this target to be programmed, so that your call can be routed to your secretary or someone within your department rather than the operator.

5. Check your messages frequently, and return calls promptly, as promised.

6. Don't hide behind voice mail. It is not intended as a call screening device. It should be used as back up when there is no one available to personally take a call.

7. Learn to use the more sophisticated features that your voice mail system probably offers. These tools can be of great benefit when sending messages to internal users. Did you know that your voice mail system probably can:

- Indicate the date and time your message was received.
- Allow you to record a message and program it for delivery at a future date and time.
- Mark a message as "urgent."
- Prohibit a message from being forwarded to anyone else.
- Set up lists of users (usually called distribution lists) that you message frequently so that you can send the same messages to groups of users.

Preparing a Message for Your Callers

For the most part, use the same principles you would use if actually using the telephone, but with one difference. I recently called someone who has a voice mail service. When I got through, a recording barked out, "Start your message now." Maybe this was rude, but I went ahead with my prepared message. I was just about finished when the voice interrupted with, "Message complete. Thank you for calling. Bye," followed by a loud CLICK. Without warning I was cut short with no chance to review or re-record it.

If you have an answering machine or voice mailbox that has a single message capacity that is shorter than usual (30 seconds or less), add some type of warning in your recorded introduction. This will allow callers to better prepare and condense their points if their messages are longer than normal. Otherwise, try the following examples after tailoring them to your company's needs and personality.

General company operator:

"Thank you for calling ABC Company. Our offices are open Monday through Friday, from 8:00 a.m. - 5:00 p.m. Central Standard Time. Please leave your name, a brief message, and a phone number and the appropriate person will return your call as soon as possible. Again, thank you for calling ABC Company."

Or for an individual:

"This is Bob Jones. I'm not available to take your call in person at this time. However, your call is very important to me. If you leave your name, a phone number, and a detailed message, I'll return your call promptly. If your call needs immediate attention, please dial "0" to reach my assistant, Ellen Roth."

Or more specialized:

"This is Bob Jones. I'll be away from my desk until 3:00 this afternoon. Please leave your name, a phone number, and a detailed message, and I'll return your call promptly. If your call needs immediate attention, please dial "0" to reach my assistant, Ellen Roth."

When writing your message, always remember to keep it in the positive. Here are some examples of positive points you might want to include as you tailor your message to your specific business situation:

- **When you are open (not when you are closed)**
- **If you would . . .**
- **Please leave . . .**
- **Promptly**
- **Special holiday greetings**

If for some reason you must shut down when you are usually open for business, take the time to record a special message. It should let any callers know exactly why you are closed and when you will be available again. For instance, some businesses close the day after Thanksgiving while others do not. In this situation, the following message might be appropriate:

"Thank you for calling the ABC Company. Our offices are closed in observance of the Thanksgiving holiday (Yes, "closed" is a negative so let's make it more positive with the next phrase) so our staff can spend more time with their families. Our offices will reopen on Monday, November 28th at 8:00 a.m. Central Standard Time. Please leave your name, a brief message, and a phone number so the appropriate person can return your call when our offices reopen. Everyone at the ABC Company wishes you a safe holiday weekend."

It is all right to be creative, but do not go overboard. Just as in answering a call, this is not the place to mention a sale, unless the majority of callers are looking for this information or there is a special circumstance. For example:

"Thank you for calling Best Furniture. We are closed today for our annual inventory. We will reopen tomorrow at 8 a.m. with everything marked down to move. If you need to leave a message . . ."

Your voice and personality are the prime elements that will make the recording memorable and let callers know that, even though they have reached an answering service, their calls are still important to your company. When recording, pump up your energy level an extra notch and, of course, don't forget to smile!

Leaving a Message

When calling another person, always be prepared for the time when you will reach voice mail or an answering service. Be prepared to speak and leave an effective and complete message. Studies have shown that as high as 65% of business calls involve the one-way transfer of information. Leaving complete voice mail messages can often eliminate the need for a return phone call. Or, it can help to ensure that the party you are calling knows exactly what you need when they do return your call. Include the following in your information:

- **Date and time of the call**
- **Your first and last name**
- **Your telephone number**
- **Your company name**
- **A good time to return your call**
- **Purpose of the call, in detail, including the level of urgency**

Actually, I often prefer to leave a recorded message over one taken by an employee (unless, of course, they have read this book). With the recording, the receiver has the extra advantage of hearing my tone of voice which provides a clearer reference as to the meaning behind what I am saying. Plus, there is no room for written error. For example:

"Hello, Rebecca. This is Tony Hitt with AIM in St. Louis. It's 2:00 on Monday afternoon. I need to get the specifics for the Atlanta project no later than noon tomorrow. I can be reached at 314-555-1234 until 6:00 today or after 8:00 in the morning tomorrow. Thank you."

By leaving this message instead of hanging up or just leaving my name, Rebecca will be able to prepare a return phone call and get the required information to me on time. An unimaginable amount of time has been saved. If I had just left my name and phone number, Rebecca might have returned my call, but without the needed information. This means another round of unnecessary phone calls and possibly a missed deadline.

Always leave your number, even if you think the other person has it. Today's technology allows callers to retrieve their messages and return calls from practically anywhere in the world. If Rebecca gets my message, without a phone number, from some place other than her office, she might have to wait until she returns to the office to look it up -- more needlessly lost time.

Voice mail can also be used to get around call screening (see Chapter 50). If you cannot get through to someone due to secretarial screening, ask the operator to transfer you directly to the person's mailbox where you can leave a detailed message.

CHAPTER 44

About Teleconferencing

Sometimes the simplest solutions are at your fingertips. Teleconferencing is one of those. It allows more than one person or location to share a single call. For example, from my office I could call my attorney and my accountant, and the three of us could talk simultaneously without scheduling a face-to-face meeting. From my office in St. Louis, I can call our trainers in various cities around the country to discuss new policies and procedures.

Some telephone systems have a built-in feature that allows unassisted conference calling, the only limitation being the amount of incoming lines in the office. Some local phone companies provide "3-way" calling that allows you to call two additional parties on one outgoing line. AT&T will also provide operator assistance in making a conference call. One disadvantage is that you will need to call the operator before the conference call with the names and numbers of each individual who will be involved in the call, and the time of the hook-up. The advantage is that you can have as many people as you want on a single line with almost perfect clarity. At the time this book went to press, the charge was generally in the $10 range for each person plus $ .35 per minute for the time of each call to each location. You can save some money by setting up the conference call yourself. AT&T charges a $15 fee that allows you to set up all the connections yourself.

This type of teleconferencing can be an extremely cost effective way to deliver the same information to a large group of people while still having the opportunity to interact. I frequently use this service to call a company-wide meeting with employees in different cities, instead of sending a written memo. At the end of the meeting, I can immediately gauge response to what I have said and can allow time for questions and answers. The chance that anyone has gotten the wrong message and is misled in any way is greatly reduced.

Multilevel marketing companies, such as Amway®, often conduct motivational meetings through speaker phones located in hundreds of locations. Hundreds of associates can hear a simultaneous "live" message nationwide. The possibilities are nearly endless.

Having organized many of these tele-meetings, I can give you a tip for success. About a week before the actual call, send all expected participants a memo stating the date and time (including the time zone if necessary). Set some guidelines for the participant. Include an agenda for the call explaining that there will be a question and answer session immediately following. Explain that since the participants cannot be seen, they should identify themselves before asking a question. Also, emphasize the importance of absolute silence when someone is talking. If 50 people have radios going in the background or all decide to talk at once, you will have a fiasco on your hands.

In the event that you are a participant in a conference call and absolutely have to step away for a moment, use your HOLD button. In the case that your phone system is hooked into "Information/Music on Hold" do not put the conference call on hold. Everyone will then be interrupted by the music. A possible solution would be to use the MUTE button which is available on most phones. That way you can temporarily leave the tele-meeting and handle another pressing issue without disturbing everyone else.

CHAPTER 45

Telephone Cost Cutting

The most effective way to reduce telephone expense is by lowering the cost of long-distance service. Choosing the correct long-distance company and plan can save your company big dollars. Depending on the size of your organization -- thousands of dollars can be saved over a year. Because of the potential savings, some companies I have talked to go so far as to have a staff person who is responsible for researching long-distance trends and making sure the company is making the best possible long-distance choices.

Even after you have made your decision on a particular plan or package, keep up with the changes. Review your long-distance carrier on a regular basis. Plans change -- and most companies do not call you back to show you how you can pay them less!

NOTE: Who is your long-distance carrier? Just dial 1-700-555-1212 and a recording will tell you.

Here are some other cost-cutting ideas:

• **If your company has an incoming WATS(800) line, make sure callers are not spending too much time on hold.** A three or four minute hold can cost $1 before you even take the call! Just think of the additional expense in a year's time. In most cases, taking a number and returning the call will save money, and the rates for the return call will be less expensive than the "800" charges.

• **Make sure your staff realizes that WATS(800) calls are paid for by the minute.** I am surprised at the fact that many employees do not realize that someone has to pay for "800" calls. We have been conditioned to think "800" means FREE. If your company has more than one location, or if people are often calling in from the field, shorter and better planned calls will reduce telephone expense even further.

• **The same is true with outgoing WATS lines.** Again, many people incorrectly believe that these calls are also FREE. Make sure everyone in your organization realizes that your company pays for all WATS calls. When placing a long distance call, determine if the WATS lines are better than standard rates and act accordingly.

• **Audit telephone bills.** Make a habit of confirming that the calls that appear on your organization's bill were actually made by persons inside your company. Telephone companies' billing systems are not infallible. Also confirm that all calls are business-related and that any personal calls are billed directly to the employee. The time that this simple procedure takes each month will more than pay for itself by the end of the year.

CHAPTER 46

Simple Time Management

You may be wondering why time management is being addressed in this book.

The majority of people who use the telephone have additional responsibilities. The way we accomplish, or fail to do these other work assignments affects the way we feel about our job in general and our attitude. If you are organized and getting everything accomplished, you tend to feel more confident and less stressed.

Several years ago, I was asked to give a speech on time management. At the time I had barely been exposed to the phrase, let alone instructed anyone on the specific principles. With my speech only one week away, my back was against the wall. It was time to learn all I could about time management.

As I read every book I could get my hands on, I found as many complex theories as I found books. Each one had a slightly different twist, and each seemed fairly difficult to carry out in day-to-day business. I started thinking about the activities I had to cram into each day. What would be the most practical method -- a system I could and would use -- for accomplishing everything on a daily basis? The result was the "ABC's and 123's" of time management.

Even though the system is extremely simple, it has withstood the critical eyes of the most discriminating time management consultants. Yes, there are books, seminars, and entire college courses available on the subject. You can learn as much as you desire on the topic. Unfortunately, it will take you years to learn all of the theories. Since you are looking for better ways to manage your time, try my simplified method:

1. **Buy a tablet of paper.** I prefer a standard size yellow, legal pad.

2. **Make a list of everything you need (or want) to do.** I mean everything! Think of it as a brainstorming session. I include personal as well as business responsibilities on the same list. Some items are as simple as making a call or completing some correspondence while other items are more long-term commitments. Some need to be done right away. Others can be "dreams" or "conceptual" points that I don't want to forget. Next to each point, write down any pertinent phone numbers or other data that will help you accomplish these tasks. Also, write legibly so you do not waste time later trying to decipher your writing.

3. **Read the list.** As you do so, other thoughts will be triggered that were not thought of previously. Add these to your master list.

4. **Prioritize your list.**

   A --Should have been done yesterday
   B -- Do today
   C -- Can wait until tomorrow for further attention

5. **Prioritize the A's.**

   1 -- Most important
   2 -- Next in importance
   3 -- Less important

Start your day working on "A1", and move down the list in order of importance. If "interruptions" occur -- and they always do -- take a mental time out and decide where they fit on your list. If they are higher on the list than the items you are currently working on, stop and handle them. If not, write them on your master list and prioritize them for the future.

If you are having a particularly good day and are able to complete all your "A" items, prioritize your "B" items and continue. At the end of the day, take a minute to go through your master list and mark off completed items. I go so far as to make this an event, using a big red marker. Not only does it feel great to eliminate each activity, but the guidance is effective in staying on top of the higher priority items. Anytime a new item arises, add it to the list. At least once each week rewrite the entire list (daily, if needed).

This is my method. Though I know it works for me, feel free to try any one of the thousands of other ideas and theories on time management. Buy one, borrow one, or create your own -- but find one that works and that is easy for you to use in your work situation. When you find the right one, stick with it, and you will see immediate results in the amount of tasks you are able to accomplish.

The owner of one of the nation's largest Ford dealerships, Dave Sinclair, uses paper plates. All important items are written on white paper plates. He says it is nearly impossible to lose a plate, while a piece of paper is easily lost in a pile. When a job on a plate is accomplished, it is thrown away. This is a unique method, but effective because it is simple to use. Do you think it might have helped his business become the #1 dealership in the country? Think about what the right time management system could do for you.

CHAPTER 47

Eliminating Telephone Tag

It is estimated that 7 out of 10 calls are not completed on the first attempt. This simply means you do not reach the person to whom you wish to speak on the first call. It makes sense that if you could eliminate this type of "telephone tag," you could eliminate a great number of your incoming calls. Think about the additional time you would have to spend on other projects.

Even though it would be wonderful, it will never be possible to eliminate "telephone tag" completely -- we do not live in a perfect world. However, there are a few effective ideas to greatly reduce missed calls and contacts.

At the very least, you should always obtain the time the person is expected to return your call or the best time for you to re-attempt the call. If the person answering doesn't know, ask them to make an "educated guess." This will allow you to plan a strategy for making other attempts. For example, if you know the person is out for the day, you will not attempt again until tomorrow. The same holds true with meetings, appointments, etc. Anything the receptionist or secretary can give you helps you make the most efficient return calls.

The same applies when leaving a message. Tell the person taking a message the best time to return your call. If you will be unavailable until 3:00, let them know.

Whenever possible, talk to the person who knows the schedule of the person you are trying to reach. Schedule a telephone "appointment." Treat this appointment exactly as you would a face-to-face appointment. Put it on your schedule and be prompt.

When leaving a message, leave as much information as possible about the purpose of your call. This type of agenda will give the person you are trying to reach a clear idea of why you wish to speak with him and the importance of the matter. It does not need to be complex.

"I need to speak to you before 5:00 p.m. today about our Cleveland project, specifically the dates and times for the contract and the quantity of the marketing materials that need to be shipped."

With the invention of fax machines, this information could be transmitted as "return the information by filling in the blanks or returning my call." Doing this allows the person you are trying to reach by phone to prepare any pertinent information before returning your call. If their schedule won't permit a return call by your deadline, they at least understand the urgency of the situation and can delegate the responsibility of getting the information to you on time instead of "blowing off your call."

As stated previously, when you leave a message for someone to return your call, leave the number where you can be reached. Do this even if you think the caller knows the number. This is especially appropriate when leaving messages with answering services or on voice mail. The caller might be retrieving the message from a remote location and might not have your number in reach. The call can then be returned immediately.

What if you do get through to the person with whom you need to speak, but they do not have time to complete the call that minute? For example:

"I was just on my way out. May I call you later?"

Respect the person's time and let him know you will only need three minutes of his time. Then ask if you can schedule a phone appointment with him.

NOTE: Do not ever underestimate the amount of time needed. The person could immediately become turned off and tune you out if your call ends up taking 10 minutes instead of the projected three.

If the person is once again unavailable for the phone appointment, leave a message like:

"Mr. Scott and I had a telephone appointment scheduled for 3:00 p.m. Would you let him know I called on time? I will be available until 4:30 at 555-1234."

It should also be stressed that if your call is truly urgent, let the message taker know that fact. If you fail to mention the urgency (for instance, "The shipment must go by noon on Wednesday") the person you are trying to reach might assume that Thursday morning is soon enough.

As with any professional scenario, a little bit of planning goes a long way. Do the following:

1. Plan your call agendas
2. Set specific times for telephone appointments
3. Leave detailed messages

These steps will assure less time spent making and answering calls and more time devoted to "taking care of business."

CHAPTER 48

Selling by Telephone

Selling by telephone is an art form. The advantages of using the telephone to prospect, or sell products or services, could fill volumes of telephone skills books. The methods could fill even more.

This chapter is a generalization. It focuses on all types of phone skills, in large part, without considering specific types of businesses. I recommend reading other books that are specifically written for sales. Even so, here are some of the basics that are common to almost every telephone sales system:

1. Know the desired outcome of the call. Why are you making this call? Write down specifically what you want to accomplish with this call. What do you want the other person to do or agree to do by the end of the call? What do you want to do?

2. Find out as much as you can about the person or type of person you are calling. The more you know about the person on the other end of the line, the easier it will be to develop rapport with them.

Rapport = Trust
Trust = Sales

3. Prepare a telephone presentation (pitch). Whether you are placing one call or hundreds, a well-prepared presentation can determine whether you make the sale or hear an abrupt dial tone. I suggest the following format:

OPENER/GREETING: What can you say to the person on the other end of the line that will get him to lay aside (both physically and mentally) whatever he is concentrating on and really listen to you? Of course, the greeting should also inform the prospect who you are and what organization you represent.

Jerrell Shepherd, owner of one of the nation's largest small market radio stations, KWIX/KRES in Moberly, Missouri, instructs his telephone sales personnel to use an opening that stresses financial gain for the prospect.

"I have an idea to make you money, Mr. Jones."

or

"I have an idea that is sure to increase your business, Mr. Jones."

BODY: This is where you explain the idea or reason for your call in detail. To make sure the caller is following and understanding your "story," you need to ask questions. These questions will not only confirm the prospect's comprehension of your presentation, but it will also act as a "trial close." Some experts believe that using open- and closed-ended questions, requiring positive answers, can help get the prospect in a frame of mind to say yes for the real close.

CLOSE: Ask for the order! Most sales fall through simply because we do not ask for the sale! There are many types of closes. My personal favorite is the "Choice Close."

"Would you prefer that in red or blue?"

"Would Tuesday or Wednesday be better for your schedule?"

Position the last choice the person hears as the one you would prefer them to choose. For example, if you want to set an appointment on Wednesday, you might use a choice close like the second example. The reasoning is that the last choice is the one that lingers in the person's mind, therefore making it easier to choose.

If the prospect answers, the sale is made. If not, return to the benefits. One last note on closing -- when it is done, it is done. Many sales are lost because the presenter is too busy making sure he is making a good presentation while he should be listening to what the prospect is saying. That might mean missing the prospect saying, "Yes, I want it!"

REBUTTALS: Plan for the prospect to say no. A "no" is simply another way of saying, "You have not told me enough yet to persuade me to make the decision you want. Tell me more."

Before the call, list the excuses or objections the prospect might raise. Be ready to reply with a firm rebuttal, but don't forget to use a "bridge" that puts you in a position as a partner with the needs and desires of the prospect. For example:

"Mr. Jones, I can appreciate why you say that, but . . . (rebuttal)."

or

"Mr. Jones, I understand, but . . . (rebuttal)."

One of the greatest benefits of selling by telephone is the numbers. The phone allows you to contact many more people in a given amount of time than you could in face-to-face presentations. Telemarketing will always be a numbers game. With the correct techniques in place -- the more calls you make, the more sales you make. It is that simple.

On the flip side, a situation all salespeople must face is dealing with rejection. An outside salesperson can be rejected 8-10 times daily. A telephone salesperson faces "rapid-fire rejection" --

maybe in the 100s each day! Prospects will generally be tougher on the telephone than in person. Above all, do not take it personally.

As with any business skill, read as many books as you can, go to classes, and attend seminars. Take responsibility for training yourself every chance you get. To be the best at what you do, it takes plenty of practice and refinement. For openers, Business By Telephone, an Omaha-based company, provides a FREE telephone sales tip line. The recorded sales tip message, approximately five minutes in length, is changed weekly (see the Resource Guide).

CHAPTER 49

Collecting by Telephone

Collections are a common part of any business. While each company is grateful for those customers who consistently pay on time, each is also burdened by the habitual "late pays." While most chalk it up to the price of doing business, there are ways to overcome almost any barrier to being paid. The least expensive and most effective way incorporates the telephone with other more traditional methods. The advantages of the telephone for collections include:

1. It is inexpensive compared to the in-person call and the individually typed letter.

2. It is immediate and produces some sort of answer the moment you make contact.

3. It is personal and allows an exchange between two people and personalities.

4. It allows you to ask questions, obtain information, and to react to that information.

5. It allows you to be flexible in your approach as the situation changes.

6. It can result in an instant agreement on what is to be done.

There are three parts involved in any collection call.

STEP ONE: Plan the call

Before you actually dial the telephone, be sure you have all of the facts and a plan for what you are going to say and/or do.

What is the current status of the account? What is the past payment "track record" of the account? Is your company "at fault" and possibly the reason the account was not paid? What type of arrangements are you prepared to propose (Just because you have a proposal doesn't mean that you do not lead off with a "full payment" request)?

Not having up-to-date information before you make the call can be embarrassing and decrease your chance of collecting anything (or doing any future business). You have to know before the call is made if there is a chance that the payment came in today's mail, merchandise has been returned, or a credit has been issued that would bring the account current. Is there an additional invoice that now adds to the account? Be safe and know the answers.

STEP TWO: Place the call

You dial; the phone rings; you are ready with a firm, but courteous voice and personality. Contrary to what you might have been taught in the past, over-aggressiveness and contempt will get you nowhere. Your goal is to find a mutually satisfying solution to the delinquent payment. Even if you know beyond a shadow of a doubt that the company is stonewalling, an understanding attitude will achieve more. Empathize at every turn, but reply steadfastly with alternative after alternative until an agreement is reached.

Now the collection begins:

1. Identities. In telephone collections especially, it is important that you know with whom you are talking and that they know who you are. Be sure to ask for the accounts payable representative by his or her full name. Avoid asking for Mr. Smith. If it is a family operation, there could be several individuals with the same name.

When the correct Mr. Smith comes on the line, identify yourself in a firm, professional, and impersonal manner (there is no reason to ask the individual how they are feeling today).

"Mr. Smith, this is William Nash of Richland & Associates." (Mr. Nash would be too stuffy. Using Bill would be overly personal under the circumstances.)

2. Breaking Screens. As you probably already realize, getting Mr. Smith on the line to begin with is sometimes the biggest challenge to collecting the account. In Chapter 50 we will discuss getting through to hard-to-reach people. In collections, the same tactics apply.

Before we try to break the screen, make sure there is a screen in place. Ask for Mr. Smith and explain that this is a matter you must speak to Mr. Smith about directly. Thank the screener for his or her assistance. If the screener won't connect you, use your discretion and complete knowledge of the account to determine how much information you can relay to the screener. Perhaps they can help you.

Avoid automatically telling screeners specifically why you are calling. This can only serve to embarrass the person you are trying to reach, and upset the debtor even more. As mentioned earlier in the chapter, attacking the screener can upset the debtor enough that you could end up at the bottom of the "to-be-paid" list.

If you have left messages and Mr. Smith will not return your calls, use your discretion and take the screener up on his or her offer to "help you."

"Yes, if you would please. What is your name?"

Identify yourself, and tell the screener that you are calling in regard to a past-due account. Ask the screener if there is an alternative person you could speak to regarding the account. If not, explain the situation with as little detail as possible. Stress that you can only help if someone will talk to you. If the lack of payment is holding up a shipment, tell them. Create a rapport with the screener and use them as an ally to get through to Mr. Smith.

3. Reason for the call. When you actually are connected with Mr. Smith and have identified yourself, it is time to state the reason for your call.

"Mr. Smith, I'm calling about your account and specifically about two invoices totalling $1128.90 which are past-due and unpaid since November. Will (not "can") you mail us a check for full payment today?"

Now, say nothing until the person responds. In sales, there is an old saying that the first person who speaks after the attempted close loses the edge. Do not lose the edge. Mr. Smith has to say something. Endure the silence even if it seems like an eternity.

4. Account discussion. The next part of your call involves discussing the account. Chances are you will get one of the following responses when you ask about full payment. Whatever the response, always initially assume that it is truthful and come back accordingly.

- **"The check is in the mail (almost a cliche now)."**

"Fantastic! For my records, I need to get the check number and the date it was mailed. That way I can watch for it in the mail and I won't have to bother you. I'll be more than happy to hold."

- **"The invoice has already been approved and sent on to have a check cut."**

"Fantastic! I don't need to take any more of your time. I'll contact the person who cuts the check myself. After you approve

it, to whom do you send it?"

- **"The company is experiencing a cash shortage . . ."**

"Mr. Smith, I can appreciate that your company needs financing. However, our responsibility as a supplier is to provide you the materials you need. I think you would agree that we've done that in good faith, but we cannot be expected to finance your company. That's the responsibility of your bank. We need to reach an agreement that is as close to the terms of our original agreement as possible."

- **"We're having trouble collecting from our clients . . ."**

"Mr. Smith, nobody realizes better than we do how late collections can tie up money. That's why I'm calling you about your past-due account. We have to expect payment of our accounts at the due date. You have to expect the same from your clients. This way we both benefit."

- **"The bank has messed up the account . . ."**

"I'm sorry to hear that. I know how frustrating that can be. I've found that sometimes banks move faster if they are getting a few phone calls. I'd be happy to call them and let them know that getting this cleared up is important to us, also. What bank do you use and who handles your account?"

- **"The bookkeeper has been out sick . . ."**

"I'm sorry to hear that. How long has he been out and who is handling accounts payable in his absence?"

For even more impact, if the person is in the hospital:

"Which hospital is he in? I'd like to send a get-well card."

If indeed there is a bookkeeper and he or she is indeed in the hospital, your card may put you at the top of the "to-be-paid" list.

Remember, some reasons, even the most ridiculous, are legitimate. In the interest of keeping a potentially good client, give them the benefit of the doubt. Never get into an argument. Check out the facts and get back to them. If you have developed a rapport with the debtor and they realize you are trying to reach an agreement that is more than fair, they are more likely to take future calls.

5. Negotiating the agreement. Part of your call is negotiating a fair agreement. If you find out, for whatever reason, that it is not possible to collect the full amount, propose a plan that will allow you to get as much as possible now, followed by a detailed plan on obtaining the balance.

Negotiate with the debtor until you can work out something that is acceptable to you and your company, but also realistic in its expectations from the debtor.

6. Confirm and close.

"It is my understanding that we can expect payment on the first invoice for $328.90 in Tuesday's mail and that the second invoice will be paid in two installments of $400, the first on the 15th and the second on the 30th. Is that correct?"

"Yes."

"Then I'll note your file accordingly and count on your payments to clear up this account. I'll drop you a note tomorrow to confirm our agreement. Good-bye."

STEP THREE: Follow up

Keep your promise. Send Mr. Smith a note confirming the agreement you have created. Not only will this note give Mr.

Smith a written confirmation of what he promised, it shows him you keep your promises and that you mean business. This could be important later if the checks do not arrive as planned. If that is the case, repeat the process to get Mr. Smith on the line.

"Mr. Smith, during our telephone conversation last week, you personally promised me that we'd have a check for $328.90 in yesterday's mail, but we have yet to receive it. Is there some reason I should know about? What happened?"

Now, you are back to the collection call. Again the pause, the account discussion, negotiating a new agreement, confirming the agreement, and closing the call. Continue to be persistent, but not harassing. If you do not follow up as promised, you will create the impression that you cannot be taken seriously and the debtor could be inclined to delay further. If you do timely follow-up, you are more likely to have less broken agreements and of course, fewer collection calls to make in the future.

The information in this chapter applies generally to telephone collections. If you are going to use the telephone for collections to businesses or consumers, make sure you are familiar with legislation regarding collection efforts. There are local, state, and even federal laws that govern what is and what is not acceptable (legal) in attempting to collect debts.

Here is a brief overview of some such legislation:

<u>The Consumer Credit Protection Act</u>: Legislation dating from 1969.

- Regulates unsolicited credit cards.
- Permits consumer access to credit information used as the basis for credit rejection.
- Requires correction of erroneous information in credit reports on individuals not in business.
- Guarantees equal access to credit regardless of sex, marital status, race, or religion.

The Fair Debt Collection Practices Act: Legislation passed in March 1978, does not relieve the consumer-debtor of the obligation to pay the debt when it falls due, but it does make these debt collection practices illegal:

- Threats of violence, obscene language, harassing phone calls, and publication of "deadbeat" lists.
- Calling the debtor at work, if the debtor objects.
- Impersonating government officials or misrepresenting the identity of the collector in any fashion.
- Revealing the fact of the past-due debt to a third party -- neighbor or employer, for example (However, you are still free to report the debt to spouses, credit bureaus, or your attorney).

Federal Communications Commission: On June 10, 1970, the FCC issued a Public Notice, still in effect, titled, "Use of Telephone for Collection Purposes." That document includes the following statement:

"The Commission has received information that interstate telephone service is being increasingly used in ways that are, or may be, in violation of applicable tariffs of the telephone company and criminal statutes." Practices alleged include:

- Calling at odd hours of the day or night
- Repeated calls
- Calls to friends, neighbors, relatives, employer, and children
- Calls making a variety of threats
- Calls asserting falsely that credit ratings will be hurt
- Calls falsely stating that legal process is about to be served
- Calls demanding payment for amounts not owed
- Calls to places of employment
- Calls misrepresenting the terms and conditions of existing or proposed contracts

As a matter of fact, the Bell System itself suggests that the following practices be avoided in consumer level telephone collections:

- Calling outside normal working hours
- Repeated calling, generally no more than one call a week
- Calls to third parties except to locate the debtor
- Threatening calls
- Failure to honor an employer's request that no further calls be made to a place of business

Another way to make sure you know everything there is to know is research and learning. For this chapter I used several sources. One that I believe would be of great benefit to any person who is responsible for collection (by phone or otherwise) is Dun & Bradstreet Business Education Services' self-study course called *"Collecting Past-Due Accounts."* (See the Resource Guide)

CHAPTER 50

Breaking Screens

Earlier in this book, we told you how to screen calls for other people. Now we are going to show you how to get through to those "hard to reach" individuals. Of course, we are taking for granted that these people who are screening you have not seen this book yet.

Yes, tricks can get you through sometimes, but there is a major risk involved that could sabotage your goal. What if the person finds out you have gotten through using an underhanded method with his assistant as a pawn? From past experience, I make sure that person never talks with me again, for any reason. Why risk it when you can use more practical and effective methods?

For example, as a decision maker for my company, I am barraged by salespeople nearly everyday. My assistant is well-trained and very capable of screening those people who do not hold an immediate interest for me. She also knows I enjoy talking to talented phone professionals.

When a telephone person "fakes" her out or assures her that he is a personal friend of mine, she shares this story with me before transferring the call. If, in reality, he is not, it ends his chances of speaking with me. I refuse to do business with people I cannot trust!

You do not have to lie. The following are some more positive and creative ways to get through a screen. I have used each one at various times with great success.

1. Become the switchboard operator's friend. Using the rapport skills we have discussed previously, get to know the switchboard operator. Depending on the size of the organization you are calling, this person might route hundreds of calls a day, but very seldom actually talks to anyone. This person is usually a wealth of information. Is the person you are trying to reach in the office? When is he usually at a slower point of the day? Is he in a good mood today? Try asking him or her who the assistant is that you need to contact. That individual will know even more about the person you are trying to reach.

However, if you are going to get to know this person, understand that she is very busy. Let her know that you are happy to hold while she takes care of other callers. And, of course, thank her by name for her assistance.

In 1987, the St. Louis Cardinals were in the World Series. I owned a direct mail company at the time and had a wild campaign idea that would capitalize on the popularity of the Cardinals while tying in with a local radio station. As I called some of the more trendy stations in town, I found it impossible to get through to the general manager at any station. Finally, I tried a different approach.

In my calls I discovered one of the best receptionists I have ever encountered. Marion Maxey worked for a "Top 40" station. She was warm and courteous on the phone, while consistently maintaining a superior level of professionalism in every area of her phone skills. I was not able to make contact with the general manager right away, but each time I left a message, I gained new insight into the station, its personnel, and the personality of the decision maker.

Yes, Marion was extremely busy, but she always seemed to have time to talk with me. Don't get me wrong, she also knew what she could not say, but she actively sought friends on the telephone -- a practice that most certainly made the clients of the station feel more comfortable.

Marion made sure that all incoming business calls were answered promptly, even though she might be in the midst of a conversation with you. Her friends became accustomed to conversations like:

"and then he walked out of the booth and -- I've got a call . . . with this hilarious grin on his face. Well, you had to be here, I -- hold on, another call . . . I guess you had to be here to really -- I'll be right back . . . appreciate the work that they do behind the scenes."

Well, with a friendly and honest approach, it didn't take long to get through to the GM. In fact, he loved my idea and it turned out to be a great promotion.

NOTE: If this person has been helpful to you, and maybe even given you information that an operator probably should not, keep her out of trouble by keeping her name out of it. On the other hand, you might go as far as to tell someone higher how well she is doing her job.

2. Become a friend to the secretary/assistant. Often, particularly in bigger companies, this is not the same person as the first operator who answers your call.

This person, even though she might be screening you now, is not your enemy, but your ally. Let her know how your contact can benefit "the boss," the company, or maybe even her. If she realizes that your call can possibly benefit her boss, she is more likely to put you through.

NOTE: Be cautious not to "sell" the secretary. Many a salesperson can tell a horrible tale of the assistant replying, "I'm not the decision maker, but I'll present your idea."

No one can present your idea like you can. This spells disaster in 99% of the cases.

3. If you have a title that will help you reach your target, use it.

4. Call at off-peak times. Recently, our staff was proposing a large training contract to a major automaker in the United States. The proposal had taken several weeks of research to prepare. We were confident that the implementation was sound. In fact, we were so confident that we began making purchases and preparing our trainers to run the project. You can imagine our shock when the proposal was rejected. I immediately got on the phone to the appropriate office to try to find out what had gone wrong. The phone was answered by a receptionist named Nicole. She spoke softly, but carried a large screening ability:

"The proposal was rejected."

"I realize that. I want to speak to someone who could give me some insight . . ."

"Sir, I have no information like that."

"I see. Would you tell me who told you that the proposal was rejected?"

"No."

You can see how easy it was to develop rapport with Nicole. Disappointed, I thanked her for her assistance and said good-bye. About an hour later I attempted the call again. You guessed it, Nicole answered again.

"Hi, Nicole. This is Tony again. I'm writing a letter to your office concerning the proposal and I'm not sure how I should address it. Is there a formal committee address I should use?"

Surprisingly, Nicole was now in a much better mood on the second call. Could it have had something to do with the way I greeted her? My cheerful, not overly inquisitive voice and personality? Perhaps.

Nicole proceeded to give me the formal committee address, and also the names of the key individuals on that committee (a little better timing and persistence had paid off). I avoided pushing her any further, thanked her, and said good-bye. The rapport I developed that day continues even now. Nicole has proved to be a fount of valuable information.

Right after hanging up, I called the company's main directory and got the direct numbers to each of the committee members' offices. I started at the top of the list and found that each of them had their calls screened by yet another version of "Nicole -- The First Attempt." Each of the screeners assured me there was absolutely no way I could talk to their respective bosses.

Later that evening, still utterly confused over the rejection of the proposal and frustrated that I couldn't even find out why, I decided to call the numbers that had been busy or not answered earlier in the day. In St. Louis, it was a few minutes before 5:00 p.m. In Detroit, where I had been calling, it was a few minutes before 6:00 p.m. Most of the "Nicoles" had left for the day. A committee member working late just might answer his own phone. Sure enough, I got through to one.

I explained my confusion, and he explained the exact reasons our proposal had been rejected. He even went on to tell me that the proposal could be resubmitted with the appropriate changes. We did and have continued to have a very successful relationship with the automaker.

It can be a lot of work to break a screen, but it can also be a tremendous edge in business. Try calling when the shields have fallen -- like when the screener might be out to lunch, before hours, or right after quitting time.

5. Set a call back appointment. When you are talking to the screener, attempt to find out when the best time is to call.

"Is he usually less busy in the mornings or afternoons?"
"Does he prefer to take calls before or after lunch?"
"Then, would 2:30 or 3:00 be a better time to return the call?"

Then confirm:

"Okay, Nicole. I appreciate your help and I'll call Ms. Hampton back at 3:00 Wednesday afternoon."

6. Use the personal touch. Speak with enthusiasm and ask for the individual by his or her first name (like you were calling your best friend at the office).

"Hi, Nicole. Is Bill available? This is Tony."

Remember, no tricks. Implying with a tone of voice is considerably different than saying you are an old friend.

7. The referral method. If someone has referred you to this person, by all means use his or her name. Depending on the person referring you, you will be put right through in many cases.

"Hi, Nicole. This is Tony Hitt. Ted Bates asked me to call Ms. Hampton. Is she available?"

Again, if someone is generous enough to allow you to use them as a referral, do not go too far. Be sure the party specifically gave you permission to use them as a referral and only repeat what the referral said you could repeat. Don't burn any bridges.

8. Leave a personal voice mail message. Voice mail can also be used to get around call screening. If you cannot get through to someone due to secretarial screening, ask the operator to transfer you directly to their mailbox, where you can leave a detailed, recorded message.

9. Mail or fax a note. Bypass the telephone completely by mailing or faxing a note explaining your difficulty in reaching this person and why they should take your call. Give them a number where you can be reached -- and be available there. Even though they might not return your call, they may be inclined to take your next attempt.

If you are feeling creative, fill out a standard phone message slip with a detailed note for the individual you are trying to reach. Then enlarge it on your copier. Fax the large copy to the individual. More than likely your "message" will now stand out among the other slips of paper, and pique their curiosity.

10. Be creative. If all else fails, and depending on the importance of your call, try something different. Possibly, send a cassette tape with a message. I know of one desperate salesman that tried to get through to a prospect for several weeks with no success. Being the creative type, he wrote and illustrated a short story.

The story was about two people that could not seem to get together for a variety of humorous reasons. Using a "choose your own" ending concept, he wrote a negative ending that would be horrible for both and one that was positive with an illustration of sunshine, birds singing, and of course, a pot of gold. He put the story in a children's book format and overnighted it "Personal and Confidential" to the prospective client. The prospect had never seen anybody try so hard to make a pitch -- or use so much creativity! Of course, they both lived happily ever after.

NOTE: When using a more creative solution, make sure your idea fits the personality of your operation. Also, know your prospect. Sending flowers to someone who is allergic is not going to get you anywhere. If you are using humor, make sure you know the person's character and personality and that the idea cannot be taken as offensive.

Even though creativity can work, it is probably the most risky possible solution for breaking a screen.

11. Reconsider your options. If you still cannot get through, maybe you should reconsider the objective of your call, or at least reconsider the person you are trying to reach. Is there someone else in that company who might be as good a contact? You might even consider asking someone else in your own company, with a different voice and personality, to try breaking the screen.

The next time you become frustrated with someone's screening tactics, be thankful instead. The best prospects are those who get the fewest sales calls. If a prospect spoke with every representative who called, it is highly unlikely that this person buys each time. On the other hand, if the prospect sifts through the calls and allows only the really important callers (like you) to get through, the prospect knows that he will hear something of interest.

CHAPTER 51

Combatting Telephone Stress

"God, grant me the serenity to accept the things that cannot be changed, the courage to change the things that should be changed, and the wisdom to know the difference."

Reinhold Niebuhr, an American theologian, wrote these words in 1934 and called them *"The Serenity Prayer."* Now printed in millions of copies, it represents to me one way to put things into perspective and handle the stress of a particularly tough day. Many other ways are just as practical.

Knowledge creates confidence and confidence reduces stress. Being more in control of your telephone communications, and being able to deal with people more effectively because of the information you have read in this book, will reduce some of the stress. There are still other factors that affect our level of stress.

1. Attitude. Abraham Lincoln once said, "Most folks are as happy as they make up their minds to be." In other words, positive people are destined to be less stressed than those who always see the negative side of things.

2. Exercise. To put it bluntly, stress can kill. In the fast-paced environment that we live in we are challenged more and more to practice good fitness habits. It is an unfortunate fact, but many Americans take better care of their cars than their bodies. It is not unusual to take a car in for preventive maintenance twice a year, yet many wait until their health is in trouble before seeking medical help. Obviously, this approach is problematic. You can trade in a malfunctioning car, but regardless, your body must last as long as you are alive. Without regular medical care, life can be prematurely shortened.

If you know your astrological sign but not your blood type, take action and learn more about how to control your own health. Remember, good health begins with you and a regular exercise program under the guidance of your physician.

The first step to starting an exercise program is to decide you need to and want to make it a habit. Exercise is nature's supreme tranquilizer. Everyday stress causes the release of a hormonal substance called noradrenalin. Not only does this threaten the heart, but it also hampers the immune system. In today's society, with so many potential irritants, this substance is very easily discharged. One of the best defenses is exercise. Any physical expression that uses up calories, such as exercise, burns up the hormones instead of allowing them to harm the body. Therefore, physical exercise becomes a prime stress reducer.

According to Dr. Bob Conroy of the Menninger Clinic, pioneers in stress research, you do not need to run a marathon each week to realize major health benefits.

"Any good aerobic routine that speeds up heart and breathing rates, carried on a minimum of three times a week for 30 minutes each session, pays big dividends."

One dividend of exercise is a lower resting heart rate, usually evident after just a few weeks. A conditioned heart does not have to work as hard because it circulates the same volume of blood with fewer beats. This not only provides the exerciser with increased stamina, but according to Dr. Ken Cooper, author of the *"Aerobics Program for Total Well-Being,"* it also offers a form of stress reduction.

"A lower heart rate during stress means you tend to stay calmer and more in control of your emotions."

Like a well-tuned engine that uses less gas and oil to run, a well-tuned body uses less energy to perform daily functions and provides a reserve for dealing with stressful situations.

3. Nutrition and Diet. Good nutrition can be a way of reducing stress, but unfortunately people tend to eat foods that cause more stress, not less. Several major items of the typical American diet, in the quantities usually consumed, can be potentially more harmful than beneficial.

Approximately 25% of the average American diet consists of refined sugars and another 40% is loaded with fats. A congressional committee on nutrition has recommended significant reductions in sugar, salt, fat, and cholesterol consumption. Their concerns included heart disease, cancer of the colon and breasts, strokes, hypertension, obesity, arteriosclerosis, and cirrhosis of the liver. These are serious problems that must be considered.

There are four areas of your diet in which there is potential harm in excess: caffeine, sugar, salt, and fat. Overconsumption of these four substances can lead to potentially dangerous illness as well as trigger physical reactions to high stress conditions. Life itself produces enough tension, anxiety, and stress. Doesn't it seem foolish to eat your way to even more stress?

Learning to Unwind

Few would argue against the value of attitude, exercise, and healthy eating habits as effective stress reducers, but what can you do at work to immediately release the tension of a hectic day?

The most important thing you can do is the most obvious, but the least used. Get away from the stressors!

I once worked for a large telemarketing firm. Part of my job was to supervise the efforts of the telemarketers. These were individuals that made literally hundreds of calls a day attempting to secure qualified leads for our sales force. You can imagine the amount of stress that comes from performing such a job.

I understood the high stress levels, but I never understood how the vast majority of the employees handled these feelings. During their break times, after two to three hours on the telephone with potential clients, they would again get on the telephone to call a friend, spouse, or whomever. If they were not on the phone, they might go to the lunch room and talk with co-workers about work-related problems and complaints. The results were always the same -- continued high stress levels when the employees returned to the job.

When you go on break or lunch, make a point of getting away from your desk. No matter how tough the day is, do not spend time talking about anything that has to do with your job. Do whatever relaxes you and takes your mind off of the day at hand. Read a book or magazine, take a walk, talk with a co-worker about your upcoming vacation -- whatever makes you smile for a while. Also, stay off the phone unless it is absolutely necessary.

What else can you do to relieve stress at work? Try exercising. Exercising at work? Most of the following stretching exercises can be performed right at your desk in just a few minutes. In order to properly perform any stretching exercise, use the following guidelines:

1. Using gentle, slow, deliberate movements, go to the point where you feel a tug and hold that position.

2. Visualize the muscle relaxing and stretching at the point of the tug.

3. Stretch again until you feel the tug. Begin by holding for 10 seconds, then gradually increase to a maximum of 30 seconds.

4. Relax and return to your starting position. Each of these exercises should be done from a sitting position and should be repeated two or three times. Breathe as normally as possible, but with your mouth open.

For the neck: Stress can settle into your neck. To get out the kinks, try these exercises.

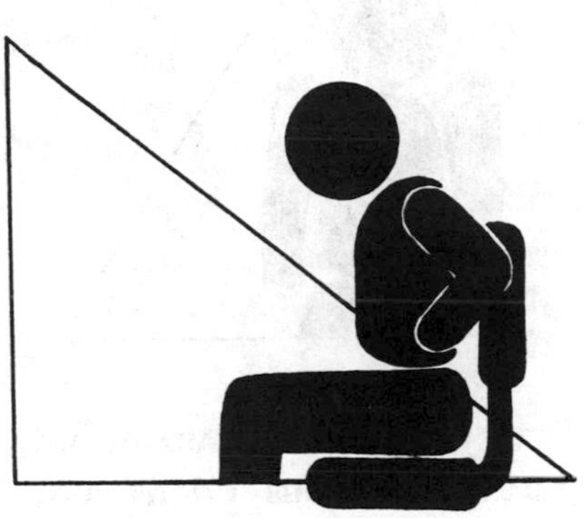

Neck Stretch. Draw your head down toward your chest as if you were trying to nibble the buttons off your shirt.

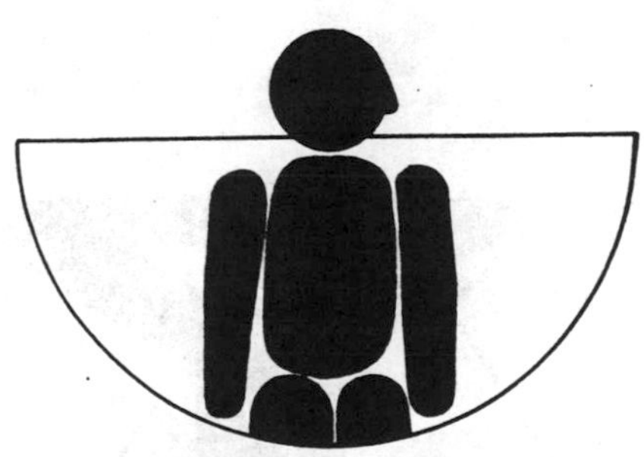

Neck Turn. Look over your left shoulder, then look over your right shoulder.

For the shoulders: If you feel the effects of stress in your shoulders, here is one way to relax it away.

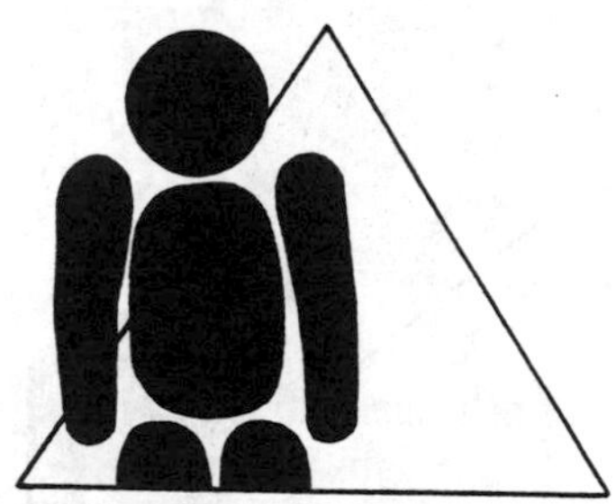

Shoulder Shrug. Draw your shoulders up toward your ears as if you were trying to gesture an enormous "I don't know." Then relax and drop your shoulders down farther than normal (The upward motion contracts the muscle, but it helps you relax more once you begin the stretching part of the exercise).

For the shoulders and neck: To release tension in your shoulders and neck, try these simple maneuvers:

Elbow Wiggle. Clasp your hands behind your head, draw your elbows forward, then draw your elbows backward.

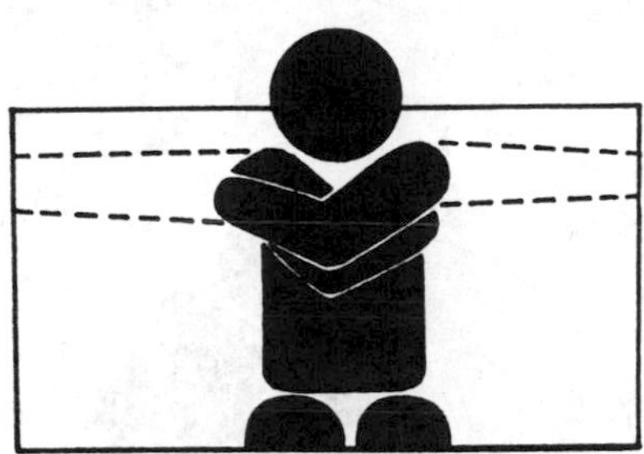

Wraparound. Extend both arms directly out to the sides of your shoulders, so that they are parallel to the floor and form a straight line from fingertips to fingertips. Keeping your arms parallel to the floor, draw your hands back as if you were trying to touch them behind your back. Then bring your arms back across the front of your body and give yourself a hug.

For the lower back: The lower back is a common site for tension build-up. These three stretches can help defuse this tension (Unfortunately, these might have to wait until you get home. They can be a little bit difficult and embarrassing to perform at your desk).

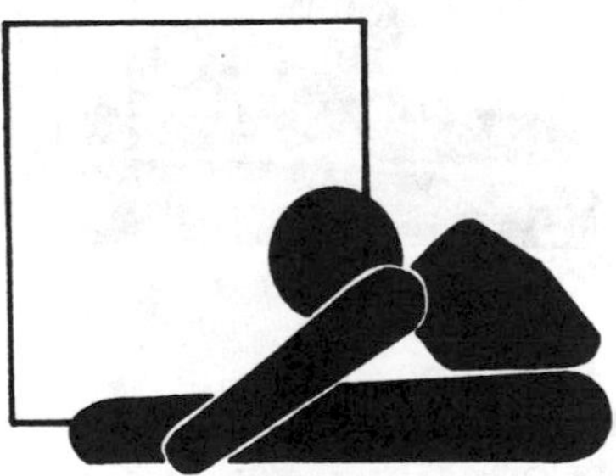

Palms Down. Sit on the floor with your legs stretched out in front of you. Bend forward at the waist and try to put the palms of your hands flat on the floor (If you can already do that, try sliding your hands forward along the floor until you reach the point of tug).

Shin Clasp. Raise one knee up and clasp the leg by the shin with both hands. Bend forward and try to put your head on your kneecap and your chest on your thigh. Repeat with your other leg.

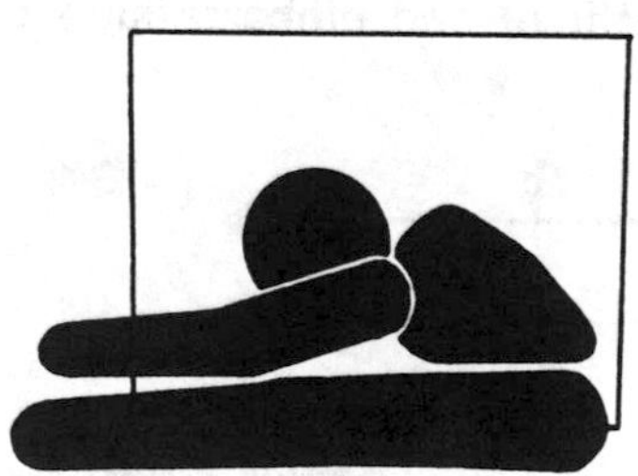

Shoe Stretch. For people who have knee problems, this is an alternative to the Shin Clasp. Extend both legs in front of you with both heels flat on the floor. Slide both hands down one leg and try to touch your shoe. Then reach for the opposite shoe with both hands.

For the legs: Calves and thighs tense up when you sit still for hours.

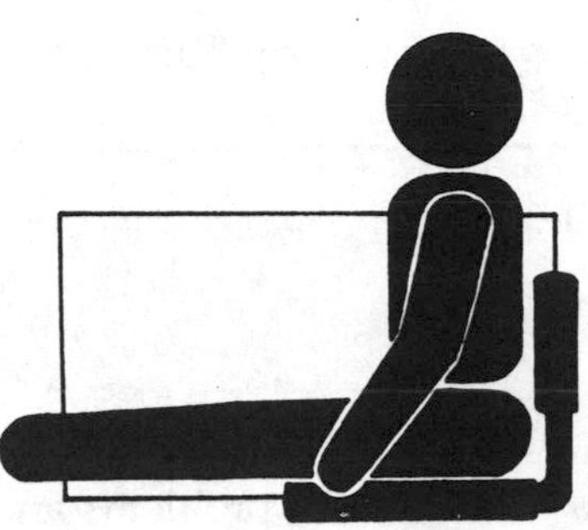

Leg Lift. While sitting in a chair, make sure your back is against the back of the chair, then raise one leg until it is parallel to the floor. Try to curl your toes back toward your body as much as possible. Then raise your leg upward. Repeat with your other leg. (This exercise has the double benefit of stretching the calves and hamstrings while conditioning the abdominal muscles.)

Remember, for all stretching exercises: tug, visualize, hold, and return.

CHAPTER 52

An Argument for "900" Numbers

The "900" phone numbers have recently come under heavy fire for numerous misuses. Most of the problems and bad publicity have been created by a minority of companies with questionable ethics. Overall, the 12-year-old service presents a list of benefits that far outweigh the criticisms.

Let's start at the beginning. In October 1980, AT&T provided America with its first opportunity to use "900" service. At that time, AT&T called it "Dial It"® service, and it was used in an ABC News Poll to determine for whom the viewers were going to vote -- President Carter or Ronald Reagan. Viewers could dial a "1-900" number, and for $ .50 billed to their telephone, let ABC know what their opinion was on the issue. The result was over half a million calls that evening.

Since then, "900" has been used for a variety of services. For instance, every time a space shuttle goes up we can call a "900" number and listen to Mission Control and the astronauts communicate -- right as it is happening. This service is sponsored by the National Space Society in Washington, D.C. Very intricate niches have also been created, including ethnically specific sponsors. One organization promotes listening to soccer games in Greek over a "900" number.

In 1987, TeleSphere introduced the first two-way services. These interactive services quickly led to the "adult service," or occasionally referred to more graphically as the "phone sex" lines, seen advertised on late night television and in the back pages of various magazines.

In 1989, AT&T offered its first interactive "900" services. AT&T specifically prohibits "explicit" services on its "900" lines.

Daisy Ottmann, the national spokesperson for AT&T MultiQuest 900®, touts the value of the new service to businesses.

"'900' is a convenient way to get instant information 24 hours a day. Information in itself is a valuable resource."

This is why I have included this chapter. I believe that the swirl of bad publicity and problems with some of the more questionable services are no reasons to overlook the value this feature holds for many businesses. "900" is simply experiencing the growing pains destined to happen with any burgeoning technology. Many things are already being done to defend against further abuses.

The Federal Communications Commission (FCC), as well as the three main providers of "900" services (AT&T, MCI, and U.S. Sprint), have seen what is happening and are attempting with great speed to change our perception. New FCC regulations require that any "900" service that has the potential to bill the consumer more than $2, must within the first 18 seconds, tell us the content, complete cost, any time or age restrictions, and the name of the sponsoring organization. If we change our mind and hang up within this initial 18-second period, there will be no charge.

AT&T caps all "900" services aimed at children at $4 and requires all of them, even those under $2, to use the 18-second intro. AT&T also offers 100% satisfaction on all children-oriented and fund-raising "900" numbers. The National Association for Information Services (NAIS) offers a free Consumer Fact Kit regarding "900" numbers. This booklet breaks the major myths about "900" and also gives us insights on how to use "900s" to our advantage (see Resource Guide). Besides publishing and distributing the Fact Kit, public service announcements are hitting the airways touting all of the positive ways to utilize "900."

Some interesting and relatively inexpensive ways to use "900" include:

- The weather forecast for over 600 cities co-sponsored by "The Weather Channel."
- The exact time, to the second, for cities around the world.
- A service that wakes you up at a time you select.

Check the Resource Guide in the back of this book for even more services that might be useful to you or your business.

Keep an open mind about "900." The possibilities are endless. If you are an entrepreneur with an idea, contact a "900" carrier in your area about setting up your own. According to Jim Ivers of Strategic TeleMedia in New York, "900" was a $975 million business in 1991. By 1995, revenues are projected to reach $1.8 billion!

On the other hand, if you have had a problem with a "900" and do not know whom to call, try these steps:

1. Your local phone company bills "900" calls. Start there, unless there is an "800" number for the long-distance carrier listed on your phone bill. If there is, call the carrier.

2. The prefix portion of the "900" number can tell you which carrier is responsible for issuing the number. Register your complaint with them. Use the NAIS Fact Kit to find out which prefix belongs to which company.

3. Ask the carrier for the name, address, and telephone number of the sponsor.

4. As with any consumer complaint, the Better Business Bureau and State Attorney General might be able to assist you in resolving the matter.

If after all of this you still do not want to be bothered by "900," possibly because of impressionable children in your home, call your local phone company. They should be able to "block" your line from making "900" calls. In most areas, there is no charge for this service on residential lines. However, businesses will pay a blocking fee. AT&T's Ottmann tells me this is because they are trying to discourage business customers from blocking "900" access with so many valuable business-to-business services being offered.

AT&T has recently discontinued its instant "900" information directory. A new magazine, *Phone Guide* (see Resource Guide), is now available to consumers. *Phone Guide* magazine is dedicated exclusively to introducing readers to the wealth of up-to-the-minute information, entertainment, and opportunity available through their telephones. At the same time, it will provide a positive environment for pay-per-call advertisers to promote their lines. Stephan Simon, spokesman for the publication, describes the need for such a magazine.

"With the astounding growth of pay-per-call numbers, consumers need help to evaluate their opportunities and avoid being taken by unscrupulous services. *Phone Guide* provides this information and exposes readers to a wide variety of legitimate pay-per-call advertisers."

The magazine boasts strict advertising guidelines. It will not accept ads for adult lines or numbers that do not deliver the consumer a genuine value for the cost of the call.

CHAPTER 53

The Telephone at Home

Why do a chapter on the use of the phone at home? Everyone knows how to use the phone, don't they? Not exactly.

I hear an incredible variety of phone answering techniques and variations of etiquette. Unfortunately, many are not polite. Why not take the phone at home as seriously as you should take it at work?

Answering with "Hello" is obviously appropriate. It follows that some relaxation of the rules is acceptable -- you are at home. Still, you have an identity to uphold just as you do at the office. I would never answer the telephone "Speak to me!" though a good friend of mine calls this his trademark. A simple "Hello" will suffice.

The recording on a home answering machine can also be less businesslike. Just remember to think before you record a humorous or off-color message. Who could possibly hear it? If you are interviewing for a job, a potential employer could be calling. What would they think of your message? Do not set yourself up for a potentially embarrassing situation.

Another difference between the home phone and business is children. Here are some points to remember about children and the telephone:

1. Teach children that the telephone is not a toy. With the advent of one-touch speed dialing, even a very young child can learn how to dial out. If one of those pre-set buttons is a long distance number, your bill might surprise you.

2. Teach children how to dial home, including area code. Explain that if they are "lost" or "miss" their parents, that you can be reached this way.

3. Explain "911" (if available in your area). Besides being an emergency line, it is another way to "get found."

4. Explain to children the way to answer the telephone.

5. Explain to your children what to say if an adult is not home or not readily available. Children, for the most part, are very honest. Discuss the acceptable ways to deal with these situations. As in business, it is probably best to have them tell the caller that you are simply "not available," even when you might be gone. This is the safest technique.

6. Tell children how to take a message and where they should be kept. Messages at home should be discussed. The "business" message book can also work well at home.

Another possibility is a method that I use with Post-It® Notes. I place these, with a pen, in the kitchen next to the phone (the most frequently used phone in the house). When a call comes in, the person answering can put the pertinent information on a note and then stick it on the refrigerator. Everyone knows to look on the refrigerator door when they return home.

CHAPTER 54

On the Horizon

I thrive on positive change. I like it even more when it includes gadgets and new technology. The future of telephone communications is full of ideas that most of us cannot even conceive in our minds -- ideas that seem to be out of a science fiction adventure. I'm going to introduce you to three advancements that are on the verge of introduction to the masses. They might surprise you.

The first is "Call Display." This technology is already available, but only offered in a limited number of states. "Call Display" allows the receiver of a phone call to know who is calling even before answering. This will allow businesses to create even more effective customer service policies by allowing a computer to pull up callers' records before the calls are even answered.

The phone equipment can already be purchased from AT&T. Computer retailers can also sell you the software to allow the Call Display equipment to tell the computer which file to pull up. However, very few states have legalized this technology. Debate ensues over the "callers' privacy." Some argue that Call Display would drastically reduce the number of people choosing to anonymously call the police -- or maybe a suicide hotline -- for fear of being identified. An example that is less serious in nature found one of the largest insurance companies in the country discontinuing the practice of answering their telephones with the callers' names in a state where Call Display is legal. For example, how shocked would you be if this happened on a future call to your insurance provider:

"Thank you for calling ABC Insurance, Mr. Cassidy. My name is Greg. How may I help you?"

The company still uses the technology privately.

The second is "Video Telephones." AT&T originally presented a prototype of this technology at the 1964 World's Fair. It allowed the sender and receiver to see black and white pictures, with a minute delay. Almost 30 years later, AT&T is not only showing us the future, but selling it. The AT&T Video Telephone 2500® will be available for purchase in AT&T stores and for use in the lobbies of leading hotels in May 1992. The Video Telephone has undergone some dramatic changes since 1964. Now the sender and receiver will be able to see full-color transmissions of themselves almost instantly. The picture will be transmitted through existing telephone lines.

Almost immediately, companies will be able to have video conferencing without the use of a camera or video system in each location. Opportunities will also open for training and sales presentations.

The initial block to this, or any technological breakthrough for that matter, will be the price. The introductory price for the Video Telephone 2500® is $1499. AT&T doesn't expect to see a decline in the near future, but past trends dictate an eventual price drop.

Just four years ago, I bought my first fax machine for about $3000 while they were still basically in the introductory stages in the Midwest. About two months ago, I bought another fax with similar capabilities for my home. The price: $400. You might remember the expensive introduction of calculators -- a remarkable innovation at the time. Now a calculator can be purchased at a grocery store checkout for less than two dollars. As prices come down, more businesses will have video phones and eventually consumers will latch on to the idea -- just as we traded in our old, black rotary phones for those colorful touch tone models in the late

'60s and early '70s.

The third, and probably the most startling advance, are "Personal Communicators." This technology could totally and permanently alter the way we communicate by phone. Using an advanced form of a cellular telephone, people, not places, would have telephones and telephone numbers! According to Bob Ratliffe, Vice President of Corporate Communications for McCaw Cellular Communications, Inc. in Kirkland, Washington, the technology to allow everyone in your home or business to have a cordless Personal Communicator already exists. The actual phone, weighing approximately seven ounces, is already being tested.

As the technology becomes commonplace, people could be issued telephone numbers the way they are issued Social Security numbers. The Personal Communicator would allow your neighborhood to be equipped with a PCN (Personal Communications Network) that would permit you to place or receive calls from anywhere in your neighborhood or office complex. As you would leave the PCN coverage area you would automatically plug into a community cellular system which currently handles over 7 million mobile telephones. Spreading out even further, satellites would enable you to place or receive calls from anywhere not covered by a land-based network. For instance, if you were hiking in the Rockies and were faced with an emergency situation, you could turn on your phone and make contact.

Unlike the "ROAM" capabilities currently available for mobile phones, people wanting to contact you would not need to know your whereabouts and you would not need to "sign-on" to a local system to be accessible. Using the "Rockies example," the current cellular system wouldn't reach anyway. The satellite network would immediately solve this problem.

Believe it or not, this technology is available now. It's just a matter of organizing the nationwide (and worldwide) execution which will take some time. Who will be the providers? How will such a communications system be fairly billed? How can it be made affordable and accessible to everyone? These are all questions that need to be answered before you will ever hear about the availability of the Personal Communicator. The FCC has already begun its preliminary research and promises to allocate enough radio frequencies to support the technology, starting in 1993.

Current plans have the PCN costing about the same as a home line does now, but there would be the need for one per person. Land-based cellular costs around $ .30 per minute. The cost of satellite calls would probably cost closer to $2 per minute. Once again, as more and more people use the system, the rates would become affordable to almost everyone.

The time will come when you will have a phone in your pocket and will call individuals' numbers, not locations. If you don't want to be that accessible, voice mail and priority paging could be utilized to screen your calls.

In my conversation with Bob Ratliffe of McCaw Cellular Communications, we allowed our imaginations to run wild. We envisioned "Dick Tracy" type telephones that would allow us to communicate with and view each other without even holding a handset next to our faces.

Then I realized that this vision could conceivably come to pass in my lifetime. For the most part, the technology needed to make this happen is already with us today. Theoretically, if someone were on the moon, satellites could now make it possible to call them on a Personal Communicator.

As exciting as these advances are, and with all the advantages they hold, there will still never be a substitute for the "human touch." People with superior communications skills will be as important in the future as they are now, and in business, there will always be a need for talented professionals.

CHAPTER 55

Have Fun!

No matter what your specific position is, no matter how many calls you handle in a day, no matter how hectic things can get, enjoy the experience. Easier said than done? Not really.

Your job takes up a large percentage of your life. Why should you be miserable in a position for which you are so well-suited? In my company's mission statement the final line reads: "At no time will we compromise our integrity, reputation, or the desire to enjoy our lives." That's how important I feel it is to have fun.

Try it. Surprisingly, it is easier than feeling sorry for yourself or dwelling on the negative points. One of the first seminars I attended years ago was given by Hattie Hill-Storks. Her seminar stressed the importance of doing a good job on the telephone and taking care of your callers. She covered all the basics including developing rapport and listening, but she also emphasized, with equal importance, taking care of ourselves and having fun. She made all the participants see that it was impossible to take care of someone else if you could not even take care of yourself.

My motivation for attending the seminar was research-related. One of my dreams and goals had been to conduct telephone skills seminars and to eventually write a book -- this book. When I approached her after the seminar, I was totally up-front with my plans. Instead of telling me to get lost, she spent at least 15 minutes describing her insights into the business. Several weeks later I called her to further clarify points. Again, without any questions, she gave me even more information than I requested. There I was, a potential competitor, and she never discouraged me. In fact, when I called that evening, I was treated not as an interruption, but as a friend. Hattie is an excellent example of practicing what you teach.

I called Hattie again the night before the book was to go to press. Even though it had been nearly six years since we had last spoken, I told her that the book wouldn't be complete without a mention of her and her work. She was the person who had inspired me the most to teach people how to effectively communicate on the telephone. I wouldn't recommend many people who compete with me, but Hattie is the exception. She has always been generous to clients, her seminar participants, and her friends. I hope I'm counted among the latter.

She shared what she believed to be the most important points of telephone communication.

"The telephone has the ability to empower others to act. That's exciting. Make sure you use that power to both your and the caller's best interest. Connect with the other person totally. Focus on the caller. Be flexible. Don't just follow the computer screen. If you do, you're not connecting. Have fun! Enjoy the process. Don't make any part of living, or using the telephone, a chore. Make it a pleasure."

Hattie has proven that by doing what we as "experts" teach, you can benefit. Her efforts warrant this page -- a page that will generate some business for her. Years later her generosity has paid off with the additional recognition she deserves. If we enjoy what we do, and are generous with our time and knowledge, it will come back eventually.

Study this book and use it as a point of reference whenever needed. Changing habits is not always easy, but to be the most effective telephone professional you can be often takes change. Don't try to change everything at once. Try instead to change one small method each day over a month's time. As always, make sure that each of them corresponds with the policies and procedures of your employer. Then run with it!

You likely have not come close to reaching your potential in your position. This should not be taken as a negative point, but instead as an exciting opportunity. Never think of yourself as "good enough." This self-imposed obstacle is what holds many people back. Just as they are stretching to the limits and reaching higher achievements, this mental boundary springs up and stops their progress in its tracks.

"Good enough" is when service slips and customers complain. Remember, when a person's mind is stretched, it will never go back to its original dimensions. Challenge yourself to be the best and watch it become contagious with the people around you. Be giving of your new knowledge at every opportunity, and let your co-workers know about *"Positive Impressions"* and how it has helped you.

Find out today how much easier your job can be when you're organized, prepared, and have the confidence to handle any situation. You now have the skills to do it and to take total control of your job no matter what is thrown at you. Start with the phone -- most of your clients do!

This is only the beginning of your success. Use the Resource Guide in this book -- in conjunction with your local bookstores and libraries -- to continue to build specific skills that you still need to improve. The final page of this book is devoted to other teaching aids included in the *"Positive Impressions"* series. Also consider ordering our newsletter. Continue your commitment to excellence by keeping up-to-date on new technology and trends in telecommunications.

Much of the information contained in this book has been gathered from the comments and experiences of fellow telephone professionals, like yourself, who have gladly passed it on to me. I would like to hear your ideas and what you're doing to make callers feel appreciated and special. Maybe you have a story about a unique situation that you experienced, but that the book didn't mention. Whatever your contribution, I'm interested. Even if you decide not to subscribe to our newsletter, jot me a note with your comments on our book and I'll add you to my mailing list. I'll let you know when I'm going to be in your area or if I might have something that responds specifically to your situation.

There will never be a reason that you can't be the best at whatever you choose to do. Live this challenge and take care.

A. W. (Tony) Hitt
Tony Hitt & Company, Inc.
514 Earth City Expressway, Suite 223
St. Louis, Missouri 63045

Resource Guide

The following listing of manufacturers, vendors, and consultants is available to provide you with additional details on specific subjects. Each listing is not necessarily recommended nor endorsed by the author.

AUTOMATED ATTENDANT/VOICE MAIL SYSTEMS:

AT&T	*908-658-6000*
Audiocom	*800-272-0555*
	305-825-4653
Digital Sound	*805-566-2000*
Dytel	*708-519-9850*
Electronic Telecommunications	*415-828-2880*
Granite Telecom	*603-644-5500*
Octel	*408-942-6500*
Rolm	*203-849-6000*
SpeechSoft	*609-466-1100*
Tigon	*800-962-2330*
Viking Electronics	*715-386-8861*
VMX	*800-284-4VMX*

BOOKS OF INTEREST:

Collecting Past-Due Accounts
Dun & Bradstreet Business Education Services &
National Association of Accountants
Dun & Bradstreet Corporation
100 Church Street
New York, NY 10007

Power Talking: 50 Ways to Say What You Mean and Get What You Want
George R. Walther
Available in bookstores or by contacting Mr. Walther at:
6947 Coal Creek Parkway, Suite 100
Renton, WA 98059 *206-255-2900*

99 Ways to Sell More by Phone
Art Sobczak
Telephone Selling Report
5301 South 144th Street
Omaha, NE 68137 *402-895-9399*

CALL MANAGEMENT SOFTWARE:

Sidekick 2.0
Borland *408-438-5300*

PakRat 4.0
Polaris *619-674-6500*

DIRECTORIES:

Haines ® Criss-Cross® *800-582-1734*
R. L. Polk *816-756-0425*

FAX MACHINES:

Canon	*516-488-6700*
Murata	*214-403-3300*
Pitney Bowes	*203-356-5000*
Savin	*203-967-5000*
Sharp	*800-BE-SHARP*
	201-529-8200
Toshiba	*714-583-3000*

HEADSETS:

ACS	*800-538-0742*
	408-438-3883
CommuniTech	*708-439-4333*
Hello Direct	*800-444-3556*
	408-972-1990
Plantronics	*800-544-4660*
	408-426-5868

ADVERTISING ON HOLD:

Capital GBS Communications	
Advertising on Hold	*314-961-4581*

INFORMATION ON HOLD:

Positive Impressions On Hold	*314-298-9500*
TAP Sold on Hold	*800-777-0898*
	214-404-1000

INTERNATIONAL CALLING ASSISTANCE:

AT&T	*800-874-4000*
MCI	*800-444-2222*
US Sprint	*800-877-4646*

LONG DISTANCE SERVICES:

AT&T	*800-222-0400*
MCI	*800-444-2222*
US Sprint	*800-877-4646*

ORGANIZATIONS:

Customer Service Institute	*800-726-5274*
	301-585-0730
International Customer Service Assoc.	*312-321-6800*
National Association of	
Information Services	
FREE 900 Fact Kit	*800-787-NAIS*

PUBLICATIONS:

Cellular Sales & Marketing Newsletter	*703-742-9696*
Customer Service Newsletter	*800-726-5274*
	301-585-0730
Inbound/Outbound Magazine	*800-LIBRARY*
	212-691-8215
Service Edge Newsletter	*800-328-4329*
Mobile Office Magazine	*818-593-6100*
Phone Guide Magazine	*800-733-3606*

Teleconnect Magazine	*800-LIBRARY*
	212-691-8215
Telephone Selling Report Newsletter	*402-895-9399*
Tony Hitt's Telephone Lines	*314-298-9500*

TELECONFERENCING:

AT&T	*800-544-6363*
Darome	*800-DAROME-1*
MCI	*800-475-4700*
US Sprint	*800-669-1235*

TELEPHONE SALES TRAINING:

Art Sobczak
Business By Telephone
5301 South 144th Street
Omaha, NE — *800-326-7721*
402-895-9399

Telesales Tip Line — *402-896-TIPS*

TELEPHONE SKILLS TRAINING:

Lori Korn
CalTel Communications
1162 Rosedale Avenue, Suite A
Glendale, CA 91201 — *818-548-2400*

Hattie Hill-Storks
Hattie-Hill Storks & Associates, Inc.
PO Box 802967
Dallas, TX 75380 — *214-418-6172*

A. W. (Tony) Hitt
Tony Hitt & Company, Inc.
514 Earth City Expressway, Suite 223
St. Louis, MO 63045 — *314-298-9500*

TELEPHONE SYSTEMS:

AT&T	*800-247-1212*
Executone	*602-998-2200*
Fujitsu	*602-921-5900*
Mitel	*407-994-8500*
NEC	*516-753-7000*
Rolm	*203-849-6000*
TIE	*203-888-8000*

** The above listing of telephone systems represents a select group of telephone system companies. For a FREE listing of telephone equipment vendors in your area, send a self-addressed, stamped envelope to: Telephone System Vendors, c/o Tony Hitt & Company, 514 Earth City Expressway, Suite 223, St. Louis, MO 63045.*

TELEPHONE SYSTEMS TRAINING:

Lori Korn
CalTel Communications
1162 Rosedale Avenue, Suite A
Glendale, CA 91201 — *818-548-2400*

900 FACTS:

AT&T MultiQuest	*800-832-4069*
MCI	*800-444-2222*
NAIS FACT KIT BY MAIL	*800-787-NAIS*
US Sprint	*800-877-4646*

900 SERVICES:

Here is a sampling of some services now provided through "900" numbers. The rates are quoted (first minute/additional minutes). Rates may change.

Stocks:

USA Today Money Hotline(.95)	*900-454-3000*
JournalPhone(.85/.75)	*900-JOURNAL*

Taxes:

IRS Tax Forms Faxed(2.00)	*900-860-1040*

Weather:

Weathertrak(.75/.50)	*900-370-8725*
American Express(.95)	*900-WEATHER*
USA Today(.95)	*900-370-USAT*

Index

Tony Hitt's

Telephone Lines

Don't stop now! Order the newsletter that assures that you and your staff continually make "Positive Impressions."

Each month you'll receive this specially designed newsletter that will keep everyone in your company up-to-date on current telephone and customer service trends. Written by Tony Hitt and a team of expert contributors from around the country, **Telephone Lines** presents you and your staff with the latest innovations in power communications skills, telephone equipment, and a review of the basic skills necessary for any growth-minded organization.

In only a few minutes each month, **Telephone Lines** will maintain the enthusiasm, confidence, and pride every employee needs to handle the telephones professionally. No magic tricks or gimmicks. Just work-smart, straightforward techniques that give you an obvious edge over the competition.

❒ ***Yes!*** *I would like to do everything I can to give myself and my company every business advantage. Please enter my registration for one year (12 issues) of Tony Hitt's Telephone Lines. I've enclosed a check for $11.95.*

❒ ***No, thank you.*** *However, please add my name to Tony Hitt's mailing list for future telephone and customer service opportunities.*

Contact: ______________________________

Company: ______________________________

Address: ______________________________

City/State/Zip: ______________________________

Telephone: ______________________________

Mail to: **Telephone Lines**
c/o Tony Hitt & Company, Inc.
514 Earth City Expressway, Suite 223
St. Louis, MO 63045

ORDER FORM

Telephone orders: Call Toll Free, 1-800-421-2246.

Fax orders: 1-314-298-9583

Postal Orders: AIM Press
514 Earth City Expressway
St. Louis, MO 63045

The following materials are available through AIM Press:

❐ **Additional copies of this book**
"Positive Impressions: Effective Telephone Skills"
_____ @ $12.95 $_______

❐ **The Audio Tape Program**
"Positive Impressions: Effective Telephone Skills"
Workbook included.
_____ @ $99.95 _______

❐ **The Video Program**
"Positive Impressions: Effective Telephone Skills"
Workbook included.
_____ @ $299.95 _______

ADD 5.725% Sales Tax _______

ADD $2.00 for shipping on the first book/program ordered and add $1.00 for each additional book/program. _______

TOTAL AMOUNT DUE $_______

Method of Payment:
❐ Check enclosed
❐ Charge to: ❐ Visa ❐ Mastercard

Card number:______________________________ Expires: ____/____

Signature: (Must sign)______________________________________